BATS & BELTERS

CHARLES WOOD

To my wife and children with love

First published in Great Britain in 2014

Copyright © Charles Wood 2014

All rights reserved. No part of this publication may be reproduced, stored in a retrieval system, or transmitted in any form or by any means without the prior permission of the copyright holder.

Publisher's Disclaimer
As is well known, Halsgrove have disowned Mr Wood on many occasions in the past and this particular volume is no exception. The views expressed herein arise entirely from the fevered brain of Mr Wood who remains entirely responsible for them, the Publisher is pleased to say.

British Library Cataloguing-in-Publication Data
A CIP record for this title is available from the British Library

ISBN 978 0 85704 248 4

HALSGROVE
Halsgrove House,
Ryelands Business Park,
Bagley Road, Wellington, Somerset TA21 9PZ
Tel: 01823 653777   Fax: 01823 216796
email: sales@halsgrove.com

Part of the Halsgrove group of companies
Information on all Halsgrove titles is available at: www.halsgrove.com

Printed and bound in China by Everbest Printing Co Ltd

Preface

Like the pungent hearth fire smoke that had once wisped and twisted through a hole in the roof thatch, the ancestors of Peregrine Wimble-Clatt aspired to be as upwardly mobile as the Snooks. They were two arms, really, of the same family – wanton ne'er-do-wells since beasts of burden shared the living space, a dung heap snuggled on nature's side of the door, thieves had stumps, and big fish swam in too small a small pond.
Then, at the height of summer 1685, came a kiss, a cuddle, and a change of fortune in the splodgy, water slain level lands of willow bed and bulrush.

Yokels called the ditches hereabouts "reens". Many were wadeable. Others, like the Bussex, were not and had to be crossed by "plugeon", no more than a rude plank bridge.

Attired in red, his dashing headgear fur-trimmed and worn at a rakish angle, Peregrine of King James the Second's dragoons was captivated by the strange words as he craved conquest in a lonely place. Peaty water seeped from the scuppers, the small hole in the heel of each of his stiff jacked leather boots.

"Plugeon," the basket-weaver's daughter enunciated, repeating herself, puckering her pretty lips, a moonlit twinkle in her dark, almond-shaped eyes. Loveliness, Peregrine thought, putting an arm around her wasp waist before allowing his eyes to drop to the swell of her thin bodice.

Whispers wrenched away his eyes. Instinctively, he assumed his chums had tracked him down. He was very wrong. Approaching the bridge was a sea of scythes – mostly carried by Taunton chaps.

Slamming a precautionary hand over the girl's mouth Peregrine's free flipper grabbed for the primed flintlock leant against a willow trunk. It caught a branch. He tugged. The bang was instant. A shower of sparks leapt from the muzzle, more sprayed sideways out of the flash-hole. The bullet quite possibly endangered an owl.

Pegging it to his horse he pulled his bosom-heaving catch up behind him and kicked his spurs, raising the alarm as he galloped. "Beat your drums, the enemy is come! For the Lord's sake, beat your drums!" The Duke of Monmouth's rebels, it seemed, had been fannying about getting the odd bloody Somerset nose forever. Mildly inconvenienced, Peregrine had got wind the rascals had finally decided to pick a proper fight.

❖ ❖ ❖

Under the perched weight of an iridescent kingfisher the green, narrow leaves of a willow branch trembled slightly. Instead of gun smoke, midges clouded. Mayflies hovered over reeds. Sentinel, its long neck erect, a hungry heron stabbed for frogs, ignoring the numerous water-skaters in the river shallows. The pastoral serenity was shattered by a skedaddling blackbird's "chack-chack-chack" as rowdy human voices approached.

"Egad, did it land in the river?"

"No, found it! A most fortuitous hit, Peregrine. But not good enough!"

Rosy-cheeked Sir Peregrine Wimble-Clatt was celebrating his good luck with a game of meadow stob-ball and a hamper of bottled ale in the company of a few roistering drinking muckers.

"Have another go! Wager a round in the 'Three Ferrets' you'll not wet it."

"Done!"

The stone hard, quill stuffed leather ball, about the size of the bowler's palm, was launched at Peregrine's midriff. Happy as an apple orchard pig he swished the length of whippy willow and smote the missile about six feet. Falling to his knees, squashing poppies and burdock, he scattered pollens into the breeze and began to sneeze and giggle. He was properly pickled. Being in debt to several rounds of ale was little bother having been gifted a baronetcy for saving England's crown.

Suitable for politic eels, this lowest form of hereditary honour came, in Peregrine's case, with a forgettable rider and a generous parcel of remote Somerset – somewhere high he could rot, some critics suggested. A place to watch a kite fly, said others, meaning the bird rather than the plaything likely to snag and shred on hawthorn and gorse.

William Snook, Bart. had lost more than just his greying noggin when a royal cannonball fragmented life at the Battle of Sedgemoor and matters had become muddled.

Crows tugged at the lips and cleaned the eye sockets of tree-dangling corpses. And George Jeffries, Baron of Wem, the hanging judge, journeyed by personal invitation to Snick-something-or-other straggling somewhere unimaginable in the Quantocks.

Finally to be clapped on the back by the grateful Peregrine, the judge passed sentence upon one particular, angry malcontent dragged protesting from the stone-dark, cramped, round lock-up – "a mere local rebel loyal to the usurper Duke," the new knight insisted.

Snook's hapless heir, a rope around his neck, his hands tied behind his back, prayed malediction. Beneath an oak tree at the village edge the horse was led away from beneath his rump and he kicked the air. Sniffling distress and hidden by bushes, his lover hugged a babe to her bosom.

ONE

Sir Arthur's Letter

At breakfast in the long dining room of Nettlegot Manor, the double-fronted extravagance he had built with his inheritance, Sir Arthur Wimble-Clatt dallied over his ham, kidneys and eggs. He had quite lost his appetite since opening that morning's letter. Imagining a square cut to the Taunton cover boundary he flicked his knife and clicked his tongue, imitating willow hitting leather.

His mood was tetchy. Perhaps, a rare gallop across the estate would improve his humour. He doubted it. All the same, he decided to give it a go. Nevertheless, the groom would probably collapse in a state of shock if told a horse needed to be readied. Sir Arthur reached over the teapot for the small silver bell to summon a maid. She could relay his order, breaking it to the groom gently. Then he changed his mind, deciding he had better instruct the groom in person and, maybe, fortify them both with sloe gin. But that could wait.

Perusing the back page of the pristine newspaper he learned the lofty sandstone tower of St James' church had been completed. The County Cricket Ground had an extra feature. He tut-tutted. "Now they'll damn well believe they've got the Lord's support," he muttered, accustomed to talking to himself.

His utterance was understandable. Mary Magdalene, who somebody described as "the noblest parish tower in England", soared towards heaven only a couple of streets away from the new edifice.

"Blazes, if Mary Maggers wasn't enough," he cursed and turned to the front headline only to slam down his fist a second later. "Queen Rebuffs Taunton". Bone china clinked. Tea slopped on the letter. And a kidney skipped off his plate, over the edge of polished oak table, and into the mouth of a portly Labrador.

The dog gulped.

"Good, old girl!" Sir Arthur exclaimed. The dog looked bemused. "Let that be a lesson to the Gentlemen of Somerset." The dog, unsure, resolved to wag its tail. The gesture seemed to go unnoticed by its master who, instead, devoured the newspaper article.

The drift was that Queen Victoria retained a family grudge over the Monmouth Rebellion. Hence she demanded the blinds be lowered as her royal train chuffed through a Taunton station prettified by ragwort between the tracks and cooing pigeons among the rafters. Her Majesty's snub had Sir Arthur's full backing.

His reason was a tad selfish. Even as he slit open the expected envelope with a new ivory handled letter knife his hopes had been minimal. They dropped further when he read the single, now soggily tea-stained, sheet inside:

The Honourable Sir Arthur Wimble-Clatt,
Nettlegot Manor,
Stickworthy,
County of Somerset.

April 5th, 1878.

Dear Sir Arthur,

We acknowledge your correspondence of April 1st renewing your interest in playing cricket for the Gentlemen of Somerset. However, to reiterate our thoughts noted in our letter of reply of April last, although we appreciate your keenness we still feel that you may lack the requisite prowess. In our humble opinion the reasons you cite of 'having barely anything to do during the close stag hunting season', 'playing with an improvised bat on balmy school evenings before dorm' and 'an entry in Burke's Peerage' fall short of what we as a team presently might seek.

Again, we regret any disappointment this may cause you.

Yours sincerely,

(Indecipherable squiggle)

c.c. Stephen Cox Newton (Captain).

"Preposterous. Damned, blasted arrogance." Exasperation reddening his ears, Sir Arthur scrunched up the now soggy offending letter into a ball and chucked it at the wicker wastepaper basket next to his new armchair hand stitched from the finest red-dyed, Moroccan leather. He missed. "Botheration." The maid could jolly well pick it up.

Rising from the table Sir Arthur stroked the black fur on Labrador's head. "Bad dog, Suzy." Suzy wagged nineteen to the dozen. He strode a couple of strides to the hearth. Lit an hour beforehand the log fire's generous flames warmed the seat of his lavender three-piece mourning suit. He had had a difficult couple of years.

Reaching up he patted the nose of a mounted stag's head that boasted a magnificent set of antlers. "You know, the villagers have started calling that wretched place you went to bay 'Dead Woman's Ditch,'" he murmured. His eyes drifted across to a portrait of an attractive woman in her thirties sitting side-saddle upon a chestnut mare. "I'm so sorry, my dearest." He spoke with candour.

It had been a stupid accident after the "Tally Ho!" when he and his wife had followed Bunt. Lady Maud had simply snapped her neck. Sir Arthur shook his head unable to understand the unfairness. His horse had been a boggler – prone to stumbling. Last second, on the first scrapings of a badger's sett, it had. He should have jumped the ditch ahead of Maud. Instead, it was she that had gone base over apex, her usually sure-footed mare tripping into a honeycomb of holes. "Rabbits," Bunt had said.

Incapable of coping with the snivelling of an only child, Sir Arthur did what paters did. He packed son and heir Freddie off to boarding school, fingers crossed that he would stay safe and 'man up'.

Sir Arthur, meanwhile, had inertia. Going riding was definitely not the norm. Summer billiards bored him. And August's pouring of the new hunting season's stirrup cup had lost its allure.

The blasted letter, however, had put his gander up. But what to do?

Aiming a kick at the ball of paper he had a brainwave. The answer lay under his nose. Well, almost. Gazing out across the front lawn his eyes fell on the meadow. Bordered on one side by the lane leading to the stumpy towered church, and on the opposite it sloped gently to the stream. The far end lay at the churchyard wall. Behind that was the little copper beech sapling he had planted in his wife's memory.

In a month the meadow, left undisturbed, would flower into a vision of loveliness – teetsy-totsies and daisies, ragged robin and Lady's bedstraw. Not this year. He had to be brutal. Harsh on the bees and beasties but, regrettably, sacrifice was needed. Ryegrass would choke as effectively as the grim reaper, and he would scatter its seed. Let it grow. Let it be mown. Let it become a green, paradisiacal sward. Oh, yes! And a wicket would be cut, its direction creating the 'Church Lane End' and the 'Stream End'. It was a magnificent vision.

"Darling Maud," he said, looking back once more to the portrait, "the confounded Gentlemen of Somerset can't stop me playing cricket. From this moment Snickworthy Cricket Club is born and I'm jolly well going pick myself as its captain. Given half a chance I'm sure I can give it a decent crack of the whip."

He paused to absorb the true enormity of his words. He was lord of his domain, he had Albert and, optimistically, there would be quiverfuls in due course of the young sap's progeny.

"Cricket shall be played on the family meadow forever more," he said cheerily.

"We'll need a nickname, of course. The Wallopers? The Bangers? Hmm. The Belters? The Belters! What do you think of the Belters, my dear?"

Twigging the question was aimed at her, Suzy desisted tail wagging and plonked down on her backside – hopeful it would do as an answer. Spying the flat of her master's hand, she cringed, wrong again.

Sir Arthur merely slapped his own temple. An afterthought had occurred – the need for a badge. "A cannonball ... a rusty brown cannonball over crossed cricket bats. How's about that?"

He thought it champion.

What to do with the dusty billiard room was obvious, having already laughed at the original architect plan of it being a library. Fashionable French windows offered an admirable view of the proposed pitch. Ideal then to employ the space as the changing room for teams, and it was the perfect place to guzzle lavish cricket teas.

He thought of the maid's crisp white bed linen, too. That could be used as sightscreens and billow like the sails of the Cutty Sark behind the bowler's arm. What a thing to imagine!

Opening a trunk he grabbed a cricket bat that had been resting on a pair of cotton coated, cane rod, batting pads. Once more his interest fell on the scrunched letter. Swiftly he bent down, scooped it up with his left hand, pat-a-caked it, and, as if serving in a tennis game, threw the paper ball up towards a chandelier. The blade swished and disturbed the air, causing crystal to tinkle. His target though was missed.

Sir George remained undeterred. "By gad, summers are going to be fun from now on. C'mon, Suzy. Stables! Exercise!"

The beleaguered pooch got smacked with true dismay.

TWO

Stable Relationships

It was late summer 1978 and the Bumpkin Crew was stranded. For them there would be no game. Something major in the guts of the ancient green Mercedes cabriolet had rattled loose whilst crossing the penultimate cattle grid leaving the Quantocks.

Down in Taunton native chattering was liberally sprinkled with Cornish, Devonian and a smattering of travelled Essex. Out of public sight, in the rickety pavilion, groomed and manicured Gillette company representatives gave the teams free razors as corporate gifts. A gesture of 'shave if you win, cut your throat if you lose.'

Oblivious of it being a match day of some importance gulls as big as dogs, bound for the local garbage dump, cried as they circled on mid August thermals. 'Tom', the weathercock atop St James' church tower, glinted in the sunlight. The gilded copper vane had the best possible view of the cricket pitch. And, perhaps, it was no accident that all the windows on the tower's stairway faced that way, too.

Any gust of breeze that turned Tom on his pivot also agitated sparse litter on concrete the other side of the Priory Bridge Road. Apart from the small rustles of discarded auction numbers for cattle, sheep and pigs the steel pens of the Taunton livestock market stood quiet. However, the conspicuous legion of parked, battered Land Rovers, made grubby by the local red soil, was explicable. Somerset's untidy band of cricketers, led by the schoolmasterly Brian Rose in his first season as county captain, played natty Essex in the semi-final of the cup. And ruddy-cheeked farming types formed a generous part of the fervently partisan County Ground crowd.

Among their number, and now overly self-conscious, was a brawny, well-spoken, tousle-haired twenty-something with rolled up shirtsleeves, wearing a pair of neatly pressed jeans. George Wimble-Clatt was sweating and missed the company of his two best friends. Both were currently amorously entangled – Jerzy with a scary young woman, Rupert with French wine and something new that looked like custard on wheels. He himself had postponed putting Nettlegot Ned, the prize ram, to the ewes by twenty-four hours.

Crammed behind a bench of 'see all, say a smidgen' sages in the intimacy of the narrowest stand, little more than a few feet wide, the pongy dampness in his armpits was palpable. He felt as if eyes were upon him. A sage made an exaggerated cough.

This was nothing new to George. He had put up with worse. At home his cherished ammonite fossil – a childhood discovery he and his mother, Lady Rosemary, had chipped from the sea cliff – gave comfort despite him having wanted an ichthyosaur. At the cricket, when it came to comforts, he had none.

Having had little nurture he had simply learned to cope. A free spirit returning from *Kind Hearts and Coronets* at the local fleapit his mother had zoomed Sir Robert's 'Yellow Peril' sports car into a suicidal stag on Snickworthy Steep – and no seat belt. The Belters ferret-keeping wicketkeeper found the bodies. It was just one of those things.

A rummage at the scene, however, found an almost empty bottle of sloe gin in her Ladyship's handbag. Sir Robert, George's father, swore blind she never touched the stuff. Locals, however, tittered at the irony and tucked into the pub 'special' – venison hotpot. They also muckraked. Had not Sir Fred's wife, a demure beauty, come to a ghastly end due to a hornet's nest falling down the bedroom chimney? A curse upon the Wimble-Clatts surely existed and remained potent.

At the inquest Sir Robert had tried to be logical. The urbane, sourly handsome actor Dennis Price had made his wife weak at the knees. For all he knew, indulging in her screen idol for over a hundred minutes meant her strength hadn't returned for braking.

Paranoid, George determined to avoid marriage. In truth it would quite possibly avoid him.

"Sminky," he mumbled self-deprecatingly, aware of his onions and swearing something was the matter with his DNA. He was cheesed off that the trauma of his boarding school nickname still niggled, even after ten years. Better not have children at all than have them suffer such a misery, he thought; and wondered if he sounded like a socialist.

Shaking the very idea from his head he hauled himself back to the love of cricket. The setting was perfect. Beyond the bowler's arm, the Quantock Hills shimmered and ducks now and again quacked with alarm on the River Tone. The scruffbags seemed to have the upper hand and liberal quantities of swigged cider freed inhibition, though not George's. It was far too early in the day. Others were not so particular. Raucous West Country choruses of "Somerset la-la-la! Somerset la-la-la!" swopped now again to "Rosey's army! Rosey's army!"

The intimate ground shook. In fine fettle, the sages grudgingly acknowledged the seasonal licks of white paint were little more than a disguise. They thought it not overly dramatic to suggest that woodworm held the rickety pavilion and the stands together by monkey grip. Indeed, the 'Cowshed' and the 'Ridley' stands were positively endangered. Yet what the hell did that matter on a day such as this?

George squeezed passed the bench of sages and out into the fresh air. He could relax. He navigated his way through the affable overflow of the Stragglers bar and from in front of the churchyard wall he roared his approval and clapped rough hands as the red leather ball got walloped over the extra cover boundary and into the silence of the old organ works. West Indian batsman and local lord of the willow Viv Richards was making hay, and talisman Beefy Botham yet to bat was fresh from 108 and 8 for 34 against Pakistan at Lord's.

Behind George on the other side of the wall, with the world's attention elsewhere, spike-haired Polly Bowmer played tonsil hockey, celebrating her seventeenth birthday romantically somewhere of her own choice.

On the wrong side of the river was Polly's best friend, Bridey – already a non-coping single mum wringing red-raw, detergent spoiled hands. Cursing the social. Anguishing where to get a loan against next month's benefit. Filling in rehousing forms. Never leaving the battered door on the latch for fear of further bruises from her ex.

Her snot-nosed toddler, left to play in the small space between the scratched council flat front door and pavement, sucked the ear of a large, soft toy and bashed both a dead washing machine and a knackered Datsun car engine with a plastic sword. Potted primulas, gifts from Polly, had been beheaded and mashed.

No bucolic Avalon, here it was just catfight, dog mess rough – unsuitable for delicate flowers. Honey monsters scolded screaming prams of tears. Goaded dogs ate postmen except on dole cheque day. And cars on bricks had lost wheels to shady deals.

A buddleia obscured a rusty oil drum, a wicket splodged in flaking white paint. But that was from long ago cricket games. Now plastic bags snagged. Scrunched lager cans littered. And deft genders dallied sprinkling baccy to fashion roll-up ciggies or, with the inclusion of crumbled dope, the outstanding accomplishment of three-skin spliffs. That is just how things were on the large estate of booze, fags, and worse.

It had also been Polly's home before the flying vodka bottle her mum hurled at her dad, the police already tut-tutting in the sitting room. Polly had cowered. A set of brass balancing scales and oodles of small lumps wrapped in cling film were harvested and put in plastic bags as was the fascinating leafy growth vibrant under lamp heat in her bedroom cupboard.

Gareth and Chrissie, Polly's foster parents, kept reminding her life had much more to offer and that she was different. But, of course, they would say that as their cramped safe semi, behind a clipped privet hedge, was at the posher end of a long, grey road. Space was needed if she was ever to follow any inkling of a leaning. Given certain boundaries, and because she could name most of the flowering plants in the park – the common names mind, not their poncey Latin ones – they had the good sense to grant it her.

Today, she should have been at work but had bunked off. Shifting spider plants and bags of peat at the garden centre seemed less attractive than Ollie. Acne afflicted and aroused by the metal bead of Polly's illicit tongue piercing, he squeezed the ripe plums beneath her Stranglers T-shirt, leaving off to fumble with the top button of her fashionable army pants.

Her response was immediate. "No way!" she squeaked.

Shoved unexpectedly backwards Ollie fell on his butt, narrowly missing a rusty cast iron grave marker. Breathing hard, he rubbed a tattooed hand through his mohican. "What d'ya do that for, Pol?"

"Dickhead. It's bloody daylight. Someone will see us."

"Aw, Pol."

She stuck out her well-exercised tongue. "Meeeeeh!"

Thunk! The leather sphere cannoned into the trunk of a churchyard yew tree and rolled to rest between the teenage lovers.

A face peered over the top of the wall. Seeing the sprawled figure, the facial expression became etched with well-mannered concern. "Oh gosh, it clobbered you. You okay, old chap? Viv rather middled it."

"'Wha'?" said Ollie.

Hiding a grin Polly picked up the cricket ball and looked up at the wall-chinning observer. She clocked the hunky features and made a spontaneous decision. She fluttered black lashes resembling a pair of paintbrushes before giving a sideways glance at Ollie. "This creep wants my virtue," she said.

"Aw, Pol."

"We really do need the ball back," said George, now straddling the wall's coping tiles. Polly gave her paintbrushes further flutters while handing him up the object of his desire. Taking hold of it he offered Ollie advice. "I'd try and move if I were you. You're lying on an old plague pit."

"Jesus!" remarked Ollie, quickly becoming agile.

Polly tried harder. She gave George her best attempt at puppy eyes. "Rescue me," she cooed.

George sighed. She wasn't exactly a vision from *Country Life*. Instinct, though, kicked in. "Righto. Give me your hand, young miss."

Solemnly, she did, closing her ears to Ollie's shouts of "Pol! Pol!"

Finding herself being pulled up and over, Polly eavesdropped an exchange of words. "Ere, what you caught there, chapper?" asked a gruff voice.

"A damsel in need. I'm being very chivalrous. Please, don't tell the stewards."

"Okay, Lancelot. A damsel? Bugger, looks more like you've poached a squab to me."

There were bawdy taunts as Polly was lowered gently to the ground. She had made her first entrance to a cricket match. On cue, the crowd erupted and she was forgotten. Richards had reached his hundred and was waggling his bat in the air. "Well played!" shouted George removing his hands from Polly's waist to join in the applause. As the kerfuffle died down Polly simpered, stood on tiptoe, and breathed warmly in George's ear. "I'm Polly," she said softly.

"I'm George," said George flushing crimson. He couldn't fathom it. She smelled earthy and oddly enticing. A memory from early childhood flickered. Was this what Granpapa Fred had meant by "try tumbling peasant gals"? Certainly, the retort from George's papa over the sherry trifle had been snippy: "Father, that's quite enough!"

George had an immediate feeling of guilt craving Polly's warmth in his ear again. The only girl to get close to him was Margie Mudworth. And flashbacks of that Easter holiday made him nauseous.

While stabling her horse at Nettlegot she had appeared from nowhere in jodhpurs and riding boots, shirt half unbuttoned. Smiling. "Come with me," she had said, yanking him by the arm towards the tack room the very moment Rupert's squeaky wine delivery van swung protesting round the corner and into cobbled yard. "Quick, before we're seen."

What followed remained hazy. Heat caused his inhibition to vanish as mysteriously as sea fret. He remembered a sweet smell of flowers and clammy skin. The fumbling. Her wet mouth on his. The touching of tongues. The panting. His caveman urge. Ignoring the toppling tin of whitewash as her jodhpurs fell below her knees. Before he could bare his own backside the tack room door had flown open to reveal his papa holding a riding crop. Peering over his shoulder Rupert looked scared.

Words of wrath seared from Sir Robert. "What the hell do you think you're doing, boy? That's the daughter of a radical. If stabling her nag isn't enough." There was a momentary pause to gulp air. "In fact, both she and the nag can just bugger off. Sod the damned rent."

In mid act of covering her decency, Margie let out a wail.

"Move young lady!"

Pouting, opening and closing her mouth struggling for something to say Margie resembled a guppy.

"Miss Mudworth? Move!"

"As for you, George, if this affects your A-levels you're for the high jump. GOT IT? The sooner you're back at that public school of yours the better.

"Now both of you get out of my sight."

George had also wished she would vanish over the horizon. Pity was Jerzy had made Margie Mrs Bobowski. Which in George's mind was mystifying.

"You okay?" Polly's warm breath tickled his ear. Strange giddiness overcame him. George desperately struggled for something to say. "I'm … a … a Belter," he blurted.

"You sure are."

"I don't mean … I mean I play for Snickw…"

Polly flashed her eyes and gave him her full appraisal. "And you're bloody posh, too."

"Sor-ry."

His awkwardness abruptly returned. He wanted to tell her about Nettlegot, of him being captain of Snickworthy, and of the delightful cricket pitch with its dandelions, buttercups, clover and exasperating molehills. And about his childhood bamboo-poled fishing net used to recover balls from the stream. He thought better of it. Instead, he began wrestling with his emotions and worries, becoming aware of Polly's head tilted one way then the other as she tried to gauge him.

Sod it, he thought. As though leaping from a high branch of the copper beech tree at home, he took the plunge. "Er, fancy watching the match with me for a bit?"

"Wha'? Watch CRICKET? Don't be so fff..." A furrow appeared on George's forehead. His mouth fell open. He closed it biting his bottom lip. He shut his eyes, pained. Polly made a rapid recalculation. "Ummm, okay."

"Really? That's so ... Oh, bloody Haggis!"

Richards was out – a full-bloodied drive brilliantly caught by the Scottish-born, and recent England skipper, Mike Denness. Fending off a mobbing from his teammates he began to fuss over a grass stain on his immaculate whites. Richards dragged himself slowly back to the hutch, 116 runs to his name.

"Oooo, that was good, wunnit?"

"No, it wasn't, Polly. It was very, very bad. I only hope it doesn't cost us when Essex take on the run chase."

The words proved prophetic. If two batsmen are set, Taunton, almost impossible to defend with its fast outfield and short straight boundaries, can produce nail-biters. Things went true to form. 288 looked gettable. After losing Haggis to a snaffle by Skid Marks, the Middle Chinnock farmer's son, in the first over bowled by Dredge, the Demon of Frome, Essex advanced steadily. Gooch flexed his blacksmith's forearms. The grafting gnome, the Essex skipper Keith Fletcher, with shuffling feet and tangled pads, improvised delicately. South African McEwan drove imperiously. At 246-4 the scruffbags were becoming desperate when relief flooded the muttering, anxious crowd.

"'Wow!" exclaimed George.

"Was that good?" asked Polly.

"Yes, absolutely marvellous." George beamed at her. Botham had entered the fray, achieving a brilliant run out. And before the crowd could settle he had caught and bowled the Gnome. Another run out followed. 246 for 7. By now Polly was engrossed.

"Are Somerset going to lose?" she asked after an Essex bat had thumped Botham for a brace of consecutive boundaries. Voicing his fear, George got drowned out by an almighty roar. Beefy had reaped revenge, shattering the stumps. Two overs remained of the match. Essex, two wickets in hand, remained slight favourites. The tension was palpable. "I feel all sweaty," said Polly. "It's so great."

"It really isn't," George replied. He got a friendly nudge and blushed. He gave a slight cough. "Let's hope Joel delivers the goods."

After completing his final over the West Indian bowling ace Joel Garner twisted a tourniquet, going for not a lot. "Six feet eight inches and the best toothy grin in the game," said George nodding in the direction of the giant bowler. "We call him 'Big Bird'. He's a legend."

Polly squeezed George's arm. "He looks a lovely bird, but I didn't see him get a wicket." George laid a fist on his forehead. Tension.

Six balls left, 12 runs wanted, and Captain Rose handed the cherry to the Demon of Frome, Bert to his scruffbag teammates.

"Look over there, Polly," said George pointing. "You see those people chewing their nails. That's Colin Dredge's enormous family."

"They all seem very nervous."

George nodded agreement and put a hand over his eyes. Off a short run the Demon slung the first ball down in his ungainly catapult action, the process neither fluid nor rhythmic. The delivery was nurdled for a single. George rubbed both his hands down the sides of his jeans. His palms had become a clammy. "Could be worse," he commented, relieved. Polly gave him a sideways glance.

The ball second got wellied. "Christ, four!" The restlessness in the crowd was palpable.

The third ball knocked back the middle stump of Essex number nine, the affable Ray East who earlier in the day had disturbed Botham's furniture with a slow, straight one. "Dredge, you beauty!" George celebrated by giving Polly a thump on the arm.

"Oww."

He apologised, then realised she was beaming up at him. He grinned back. "You know, I think we might win after all."

Essex's ten and jack – keeper Smith and blonde England bowler 'JK' Lever – met mid wicket for a quick conflab and were then handed a present of abundance. For the Somerset supporters the over's fourth ball was the stuff of nightmare. The umpire stuck out his right arm.

"No-ball! Hellfire! Oh you bloody idiot! ... Oh, Christ almighty, no!" The screeches of George met those of the multitude as a scruffbag fielder hurled overthrows to compound matters. The sages on benches chuntered something about death wishes. Polly held an expression of pure bewilderment.

With only four runs needed off three balls Essex were now very much the favourites. Next ball brought a swing and a miss. The scales tilted again. Off the sixth ball, produced another scampered single. Courtesy of the no-ball one delivery remained. Three runs were needed. The whole ground went into a state of prayer. Captain Rose, with the obvious exception of The Demon, deposited each and every scruffbag player, including keeper Derek Somerset Taylor, on the boundary. And it was transparent each willed the ball not to come their way.

George, his gaze fixed on The Demon, mused aloud. "If he bowls another no-ball his family will hang him here. If not, I will."

"Really?"

"Shut up, you know what I mean."

"Meeeeh! Is that old bloke in front of us having a heart attack?"

"Please, shut up. God, here we go." In the descended hush The Demon lumbered in from the end of his run – an albatross trying to take wing.

Contact. The ball got bludgeoned out towards Rose. He dithered. Perhaps he had not seen it. An eternity passed. Fans bayed. Players Roebuck, Slocombe, Burgess and Breakwell panicked and froze. Richards tried to command but his shouts of "Run, man, run!" where lost to the howling of the River Stand. Rose, though, started to move, gaining momentum from slow motion and legs of rubber. The batsmen had already taken a single and had crossed for another.

Scores now level, Rose swooped the ball up at the first attempt and hooned it in the general direction of the wicket. The orb flew well over a yard off its true target as Smith pelted blade outstretched towards his ground. Grabbing ball in glove Taylor, belying his years, twisted and dived with the elegance of a Red Ruby bullock at the stumps, shattering them akimbo. Umpire Evans had a quick shufti at umpire Jepson and raised a rapid finger.

The scruffbags had won, albeit just, having lost fewer wickets in their innings.

In a mass frenzy of jubilation George made a spluttering sound resembling 'Good old Somerset', and started to cry. Shouting "Yay!" with each handclap above her spikes, Polly bounced up and down like a Tigger. Every yay revealed her tongue stud. Spying it, George was aghast. "Yay! Yay! Yay!"

As the dust finally settled distant Land Rover engines roared. And while slow sages packed away their gubbins Polly asked: "Are all cricket games as good as that?"

"Not really," said George. And although conscious of some new uncertainty, he popped Polly a question that had been brewing for a few hours. "Fancy sharing a celebratory cider?"

"Nah. Thanks anyway. Gotta go into town and find Ollie."

Jealousy raised its horns. George was flummoxed. "That oik?"

Above them on his rod Tom turned away and the air became chilly.

"Piss off, posh boy. Go get a cold shower."

Without the foggiest idea, let alone care, that the 'Golden Era' of Somerset cricket had just begun, George, alone and hurting, consoled himself. "Does not matter. She was just a squab."

He set off toward the cattle market. Around the side of the pavilion Polly watched him leave. She was smitten on two counts. "Mind out, love." A kitchen lady, puce from exertion from carrying a vast cooking pot of peeled potatoes, nudged her way past.

"Where's the nearest way out?" Polly asked, disorientated.

"Farmer White gates behind you. You alright?"

"Who's Farmer White?"

"Lord love us. I haven't got time to prattle. Ask our Nobby." She nodded towards an aged steward idly inhaling a roll up.

Polly asked him the question. He coughed, looked her up and down and frowned. "You taking the mick?"

"Nah, straight up. Who is he?"

"Was. Tough nut from the Quantocks. Cantankerous. Colder than a river trout. Poker addict. Picked the seam of the ball so much that his hands bled. Captained England and Somerset a long time ago. Somewhere, there's a picture of him riding a white donkey."

"In Somerset?"

"No, love. Egypt, if I remember. Khartoum. Or maybe it was Sammy Woods on the donkey. Now, Sammy Woods ..."

Polly had stopped listening. Rather, as the Tone melded into the Nile, she imagined a pitchfork-waggling farmer in a smock telling a pharaoh to get off his land. Seagulls became egrets. Alder trees, date palms. The two church towers, pyramids. The wondrous cricket square, desert. Viv Richards hit a six with a tea towel on his head. She and Posh Boy rode a camel, lolloping to recover the ball. She tried and tried to hold the vision but just could not. Screwing up her face she gritted her teeth, resigned that on far side of the river was another world, one less romantic to which she must return.

"Penny for your thoughts," said Nobby.

"Nothing. Gotta go. Thanks."

Overhead, a gull cried.

THREE

A Pep Talk

According to George one needed "a periscope or a talking alpaca" to find Snickworthy and its cricket pitch. High hedges of beech funnelled numerous lanes diverted every which by mossy-banked streams and wooded slopes, some not seeing the sun for half the year.

Get lucky and one encountered a deepening gash in the red sandstone where a sunken lane tagged the 'Back Passage' began. Here, a lightning-struck oak, its trunk split into a pair of pollarded limbs, stuck two fingers up at the world. Somewhat surprisingly change, when it happened, was subtle and complicated.

Although full of charm to some, 'Snicky' as it was known to the disaffected was like other places in England – unremarkable, gossipy and haunted by the trivial. Muddled around an ancient narrow stone bridge, the bane of tractors, the village endured as a maze of leafy ways accessing assorted cottages, an unremarkable bungalow, a row of tidy council houses, oddly named 'The Loop', a garage business and a scattering of farmsteads, the smartest of which cashed-in on pheasant blasting.

In addition, the primary school functioned on the principle of "catch and civilise early". Great things were offered by the village hall – even a doctor's surgery on a Wednesday morning and the WI 'bring and buy' on a Friday. The pub, the 'Burning Stump', offered oblivion. The church had long given up on salvation – goings on in the rectory the stuff of hearsay. By comparison the forge merely held surprise. The 'Prattle Wagon' from Brockcombe delivered the dailies that were plonked beside an honesty box within the old lock-up. While visits from the 'Quantock Camel', a rattling motorised emporium peddling dear basics, intermittently staved-off starvation.

And, of course, there was Nettlegot where Sir Robert's young cook and housekeeper, Joy Budd, was proud of her cricket tea. The smell of baking scones and Victoria sponge, not to mention flapjacks and gingernuts, made Lobb the Duckdog, a Border collie, drool and signalled advanced forward planning.

Her flour-dusty apron hid a frumpy white blouse and navy skirt bought from a home catalogue. She was a sensible soul with never enough time for dressing up, especially as she also kept the church prettified with botany and the pews polished. The discrete silver cross hanging from a thin neck chain, however, was an adornment of fancy rather than faith.

She observed George wrestling with a wellington boot and patted the back of her practical bob. It wasn't really her place to say, but if only he stopped his habit of dropping his brown work trousers like a cowpat on the floor and found a new fragrance he would be quite a catch – which was also how, she admitted, she felt about Nettlegot's odd-jobber-cum-gardener.

"Mine!" Barri shouted. The heat was stifling. Sweat drenched him. It dripped from beneath his helmet, blurring his vision. Yet, he'd made the decision. Had to take responsibility.

The Lord's crowd held its breath. Many ducked for cover. Others hid behind newspapers. Pints upon trays were spilt. Terrified parents hugged kids. Teammates in camouflage uniform ran around like panicked rabbits. Gauntleted, he circled the stumps his eyes fixed on the plummeting sphere.

"Concentrate, concentrate," he was telling himself. A drop was unthinkable. Catastrophic. People could be maimed. Killed, even. "Catch it!" And then he was stumbling.

Boom.

Barri blinked awake with a start. Discombobulated and panting, his T-shirt and blanket sodden. His hands were shaking. With fingertips he scratched his scalp through a mat of dishevelled sandy coloured hair and groaned. Everything was normal in the airless tack room of the Wimble-Clatt's defunct stable block.

Now Barri's clothes draped over the wooden saddle horse. A copy of 1978's Wisden lay beside the little alarm clock, battered radio and reading lamp on the spindle-backed chair. On the pine table was a bag of grass seed and a kettle sat upon a primus stove. Keeping them company were the dregs of last night's Pot Noodle, gloopy upon a page of biro circled racing odds in yesterday's *Guardian*.

Sunshine shone on a trio of toppled glass cider bottle empties and pooled on the stone-flagged floor faintly stained by whitewash. Two faded sets of footprints, one large one small, headed for the door. Shadows cast by the window's clinging cobwebs patterned the rough, white painted wall. They played upon the blade of his weathered cricket bat and a battalion photograph taken at Bessbrook, the sprawling, massive century old linen mill, tall chimneys and all, converted into barracks in County Armagh.

"Cach, I need air." Husky, Barri felt as if a badger had crawled down the back of his throat. He reminded himself yet again to prise the window open, stuck fast when someone had given the frame an over-enthusiastic slap of paint.

Boom. A wellington boot kicked the door a second time. "Barri! Get up, you lazy Welsh squaddie! It's Friday. Get your skids on. If you don't move your arse you'll miss the WI! Big Doug, Mel and Griffin are already getting the pick of the pickles."

"And I hope you haven't forgotten we've got Rookton coming up."

"I flattened the pitch's molehills yesterday evening, if you hadn't noticed!"

"I didn't mean …" George stopped mid-sentence refusing to buy into Barri's tetchiness. "Team meeting's in the pub this evening. It's Old Willy's farewell. Remember?"

"Bog off, George!"

"Open the door. Come and be civilised." George chuckled to himself knowing full well to be patient when it came to the Belters' opening bat and wicketkeeper, who, in return for paying Sir Robert a peppercorn rent of a pound a year for the tack room, was also groundsman to the cricket pitch in addition to his work-a-day commitments.

"You look like shit," observed George as Barri emerged scratching stubble.

"And 'bore da' to you," said Barri. Modesty preserved by a pair of Y-fronts, a threadbare towel over his arm, he headed for the outside tap in the cobbled yard.

George followed. "You been having those dreams again?"

Barri nodded glumly. "It was the Cup Final. Horrible, it was. A total disaster." He sluiced himself down with the cold water. "I think I'll give the WI a miss this week and amble up to the barrow and standing stones, instead. I'm sure the Bumpkin Crew can survive without me."

"Want some company."

"I don't need a bloody nanny. Sorry. It's okay. Ta, anyway. I'll be fine … honest."

But he wasn't fine. The doctor said it was 'PTSD'. There had been a bomb explosion and that was that – butcher's business. He was grateful to Reverend Clewes and Sir Robert in helping him get back on his feet. Mates hadn't got feet to get back onto. Many called it the 'Troubles'. Others called it 'Operation Banner'. What a fiasco. Some soldiers had been flown into Belfast at such short notice they had arrived with bayonets fixed. And signs they carried warned rioters to disperse – in Arabic.

Landmine risk caused the little village of Irish granite to reportedly be the busiest helicopter airport in Europe. And that after the village had once had a philosophy of 'Three P's': no pubs, no pawnshops, and therefore no need for police.

The young beggar woman in a shawl hugging a babe wrapped in a blanket to her chest was burnt into his retinas. "Can you spare some change. I want my child to grow up happy," were the last words she said. Two more innocents Reverend Clewes had consoled in the bomb's aftermath – a harrowing time for the barrack's army chaplain that was never spoken about.

Glad that both had kept in contact, Barri, though, was unsure whether the reverend, having retreated deep into the Somerset sticks for his own reasons, had also kept faith in God.

"See you later then, George."

"Don't go frightening the wildlife."

Instinctively, Barri's hand shot up to the long scar on his face. "I meant have a shave, you oversensitive twit."

Of course, Barri was going to have a shave as well as make his bed immaculately with hospital corners. The habits of a serviceman, even a veteran, never die.

❖ ❖ ❖

First to speak at the weekly team meeting was Timmy Dapling. "I like your trendy tank top, vicar."

"It's not a tank top, it's a cardigan."

"Tank top."

"You'll only play tomorrow if your mum lets you. You don't want me to dissuade her, do you? No? So, no more cheek."

"I wasn't …"

"Button it." The Reverend Delvin Clewes could play it firm when necessary and was probably better at doing that than hitting the stumps with his off breaks. He placed his black beret on the pub bench and stroked thoughtfully at his neat, grey beard. "Rookton are quite strong at the moment, I've heard."

"We'll certainly need eleven players," said George, glancing calculatingly at Timmy, now quiet with a glass of ginger beer. "Are we all here?"

There were grunts and monosyllabic replies. George decided on a head count.

"Barri, you open with Jerzy … Where is Jerzy?"

"He'll be here. I passed him mucking out Margie's stable. He looked proper pissed off."

Timmy giggled. "Didn't know Margie lived in a crappy stable."

"That's enough, Timmy," said George, restraining a chortle only for it to pop out as a hiccup.

"If Margie wanted a spaniel she should have bought one, not married one," quipped Barri.

George hiccupped again. "Rupert, I'm putting you in at three. Big Doug, you're at four. You have licence to wallop." A huge man, 'Big Doug' Birchtree, a classical singer, was the trundler of the Belters attack and, when needs must, a lusty swinger of the willow. What let him down was actually connecting with stumps or leather. Owner of 'The Bumpkin', his eccentricity and navigation were, to the rest of the Bumpkin Crew, also nominal failings. Along with Sir Robert he was Rupert's best customer.

"Then it's me, Mel and Griffin. Muscly and freckled, Mel, the feisty village blacksmith, appeared content. "Woo, the lady's going up the order!" she shrilled, and punched the air. "Wait till I tell Wellard." She meant her ginormous pet saddleback pig named after the Somerset indefatigable trier Arthur Wellard – the England player and the blacksmith village cricketer at the same time.

Griffin, carpenter, local history buff and skipper of the *Pertelote* – a problematic skiff – seemed happy enough, too, summer hay fever now behind him. His pouch of Golden Virginia resealed, he tore a small rectangle of card from his Rizlas packet and rolled a roach, a fitting end to his methodically made roll-up. "I'll be glued to the crease," he said, making Mel light up with a guffaw.

"Ah, that will explain your total lack of foot movement, you gawky beanpole." She gave Griffin a friendly shove that almost spilled him off his seat. Flakes of sawdust fell out of his short-cropped ginger curls.

"Delvin, I want you at eight to protect the tail," continued George before looking over to the bar. "Willy, are you okay with nine?"

"Yeah, I'm no spring rabbit."

"But you are a rabbit, mate," said Barri.

Everyone laughed except 'Keen Kev' Furet. "That's outrageous!" he exclaimed. "I'm way better than Willy. How come he's in before me? I've just gone and bought myself a load of new kit."

"Think that will help? You've had so many noughts you could win an Audi badge." The sarcasm came from Jerzy, at last making his appearance. Keen Kev, proprietor of Blackberry Windows and church sidesman, glared daggers.

Delvin reached out to touch Keen Kev's arm. "Don't forget we're a team. And you're part of it. Didn't I ramble about team spirit last Sunday?"

Prising the lid off a sweet tin Keen Kev popped an old-fashioned humbug in his mouth. "Thinking about your sermon, Reverend, you lost me with the chopsticks."

"Or were you actually listening? You seemed engrossed in flicking Mrs Dapling with that grubby squirrel tail of yours."

"It's not, it's been in the wash. And Mrs Dapling kept nodding off."

"Hardly surprising. Four bickering children, a new baby, and an abandoning husband now obsessed in pheasant breeding."

"I do exist, you know," said Timmy indignantly.

Delvin raised a digit of apology. "Sunday service is probably a rare occasion your mum has a moment to herself." He turned back, smiling benignly at his zealous church assistant. "Leave Mrs Dapling alone in future, unless, of course, she starts snoring. But then only one or two flicks."

"You still lost me with the chopsticks," said paunchy Keen Kev, a stubborn glaze crossing his vision.

"Fine!" Delvin slapped the table. It was wobbly. Fuller pints splashed soaking beer mats.

"Go easy, vicar," Old Willy called across, "I'm not in the mood for skivvying tonight."

"Apologies, Willy. With your permission, George, can I say a word or two about teamwork for our Kevin, here? As none other of you lot were there, maybe what entered my head will fall on fertile ground at the end of the day."

Rupert looked at his watch. "Better get on with it then, Delvin." There was cause for more laughter.

"There was eleven people sat either side of a table and they were each given a pair of long chopsticks to eat with. They were so long that it was impossible for anyone to get the food from their plate to their mouth." Delvin held his hands wide apart as if indicating the wingspan of a herring gull. "How do you think those people managed to feed?"

"Chucked away the chopsticks and used their hands," guessed Timmy.

"No, they each had to use a pair of chopsticks."

"That's silly," Timmy said, slumping. Others shook theirs heads experimenting with imaginary chopsticks.

A bulb of inspiration switched on in Mel. "It's obvious. They must have each fed the guys opposite."

"Exactly!" said Delvin, striking the table again. "Teamwork, you see. Let's have some tomorrow afternoon."

"So, I'm batting ten?" said Keen Kev, wanting clarification.

"Well, that depends." George sounded hesitant. "If Timmy's mum says he can bat ... "

"Oh, no way! Absolutely no way!" Keen Kev's outburst bordered on the apoplectic.

Mel muffled her mouth with a hand. "Drop this man now," she said in a deep growl.

"Reverend, this ain't fair," whinged Keen Kev, hurt by the titters. "The boy should bat at eleven if it's his first game."

Delvin focused on his almost empty glass for a few seconds. "I think what we need to do at this point is give three cheers to Old Willy for his years at the Stump. Just glad he can carry on batting. But behind the bar things will never be the same."

"Too right," said the Belters number three.

"Hip, hip," said George. "Hooray!" shouted everyone with varying degrees of enthusiasm. "Hip, hip!" "Hooray!" "Hip, hip!" "Hooray!"

Willy's jaw quivered.

Standing up, Big Doug cleared his throat and in his deep bass sang 'The Blackbird'.

"Where be that Blackbird to? I know where he be,
He be up yon Wurzel tree, And I be after he!
Now I sees he, And he sees I,
Buggered if I don't get 'en
With a gurt big stick I'll knock 'im down
Blackbird I'll 'ave he!"

At its end, Old Willy swallowed. Maybe, a tiny tear trickled down one cheek. "Now bugger off the load of yer. Thems me last orders."

His was a vanishing Somerset, organic, one in which a bumblebee was called a dumbledore; bim-boms, church bells; and a mole was a muddywant that tunnelled want-wriggles. For this man who had grown from the red soil folk came as two sorts – the 'bibbler' who enjoyed a drink and the 'guddler' who knocked it back until paralytic. Neither of them were his problem any longer.

Later, the pub locked and bolted, and the drip trays emptied, Old Willy admired his profile in the wardrobe mirror. The spotless white coat and cap gave him the resemblance of cricket's beloved umpire 'Dickie' Bird, although Old Willy wasn't quite as hunched as the eccentric Yorkshireman. However, the dress code wasn't for umpiring. It was for the job of steward at the County Ground come next season. Nobby was retiring.

Sometime in the forthcoming days 'Rupert Shovelton, licensee' would be painted above the Burning Stump's threshold.

FOUR

The Rookton Rocket

Sail up, the *Pertelote* was as unstable as the Belter's batting order. Lovingly conceived, she had been sawn, pegged, glued, planed, sandpapered and painted – Griffin all the while turning an ear to Test Match Special. Two near duckings in the harbour, however, and he had returned to his drawing board.

After which, having recovered a soul part on almost turning-turtle, he'd snapped his draughtsman's pencil in frustration.

He should have been bobbing about in the Bristol Channel waiting for the tide to turn, rod dangling for codling and hobbit sharks with a slimy bait box full of stinky squid more slippery to grasp than a thick outside edge. Instead, Griffin chiselled and rasped the crafted case of a grandfather clock he had agreed to barter for an outboard motor. Until the deal was done the *Pertelote* was mud-stuck.

Innovation, though, had arisen from the boat design grief. The Belters had sightscreens. Behind twin sets of stumps sailcloth billowed in the breeze. Tied to rough wooden frames they flapped a lot less than Keen Kev's butterflies as he fretted at cow corner.

He did see the ball. He scuttled into a position where he thought to catch it. A misjudgement. He trotted forwards. The ball landed behind him. He scrabbled after it, gave it an accidental boot and saw it roll apologetically over the boundary. He despaired.

"You wazzock!" yelled Mel from the bowler's end, and not for the first time during Rookton's innings. "Wellard could have caught that with a trotter, blindfolded."

The Belters would be chasing a formidable score and needed to beware of the 'Rookton Rocket'.

Nibbling and nurdling, and on occasions expansive, Barri and Jerzy had the scoreboard rattling nicely before an errata of overconfidence. Rupert unfortunately tripped when his pad buckle ripped while waddling for an easy single. His run out preceded Big Doug heaving all around a straight one, which caused Mel to stride out to bat with George.

"Think Wellard," she said to herself, for once not meaning her pig. She meant Arthur Wellard, her hero. He theorised that if a ball was smitten hard and high enough, no fieldsman on earth could stop it, and his sixes had flowed like ack-ack fire – more than five hundred of them.

"Typical," Mel said, "stick on the quickie. How predictable." Truculent, she resolved to emulate Arthur's crude science as the Rocket was tossed the ball. It was always thus – as if when encountering a woman batter the opposition had a point to prove.

"Well, bring it on, lads," she thought, vowing to be the first Belter to eventually hit a century. The plucky blacksmith knew that in the olden days of pinafores and frumpy skirts the fairer sex used to play cricket with a blue ball. Men assumed red would petrify. "This lady's not scared of nuffin," she snarled.

The Rocket put up a head of steam. But lo and behold it was all puff. Mel swatted the gentle bounce easily. And with that she knuckled down.

Then came the long and the short of the affair. The Belters had got within fifty when George holed out to long on. Not long after Delvin carved feebly to point and elicited words inappropriate for Sunday service.

Mel took on the mantle of responsibility assisted by Griffin. Crack. The ball flew to the churchyard wall, bisecting deep cover and third man.

"You've earned yourself a pork pie," said Griffin, coming down the pitch to do some 'gardening'.

"Piss off," Mel smiled.

"How about a ham sandwich?" he badgered.

"Try that again, young filly," goaded the Rocket. She did and plopped the next ball into the flabby gut of gully, who clutched-on with a bleat. "What d'ya say, luv? Wash your mouth out with soap," the Rocket joshed.

Bat under her arm she dragged herself off towards a cheese and pickle doorstop, a Joy special saved from tea. Midway, she slowed to give encouragement to the youthful incomer. "You can do it. Remember, play the ball with soft hands. Don't keep them rigid as an anvil. Chin up. We can't rely on Kev Furet, can we?"

Timmy tried mentally to adjust to the advice and prepared for battle. "Be careful, me darling!" called out Mrs Dapling sat on a rug, her newest asleep in a pushchair. The Rocket had three balls of his last over to bowl.

"Wonderful shot, Timmy!" Delvin jumped up and down with relief. The whippersnapper was off the mark with two. Two balls left in the over. Timmy faced just one.

"Stuff the gash with moss and spider web. Then wrap his bonce with vinegar and brown paper." Griffin's old-fashioned advice offered in the heat of the moment to no one in particular was unhelpful.

Mrs Dapling, distressed over her 'little soldier', was quick to tell Griffin to shut up. For all intents and purposes Timmy was sparko.

Her cheeks tear-stained she cradled Timmy's noggin. He was bleeding like a stuck pig. Blood from the head wound had soaked into his cricket whites, polka-dotted the white line of the crease and now blotted his mum's summer dress. "I won't forget this! Why did I let him persuade me? This is all the vicar's fault," she wailed.

"You can't blame Delvin, Mrs Dapling. Blame the bowler," said Griffin gesturing towards the culprit. Pallid, the Rocket wore a look of astonishment at his achievement.

Griffin continued to do his best. "Timmy really wanted to play. The vicar knew that. And we need young players. Five minutes ago you were cheering him for his first runs. Been cruddier had he stayed a duckling."

Mrs Dapling was not for calming. "He's hurt. Can't you see my Timmy's hurt?"

"I can, Mrs Dapling, but I promise you he's not needing a shroud of sailcloth," Griffin assured. The centre of attention and limp as a dying Nelson, Timmy twitched a smirk.

However, there was nothing the slightest bit amusing about him collapsing on his wicket having worn one for the team. The bottom line from the Belters perspective was forty-six needed to win with only Keen Kev left to bat. Despite the spanking-new kit Griffin was rightly not over-confident.

The Rocket bowled the remaining ball of his over and Rookton had won handsomely.

FIVE

Fedora and Pong

Tormented by his infernal secret Delvin was grateful it was almost high noon. He had killed time trimming his beard and the Rookton encounter was furthest from his mind. Pacing the vestry he roused himself with a swig of communion wine, checking the wall clock for the third time in five minutes. He had qualms. Everything was so irrational. Civilization being defined by what it forbid more than by what it permitted hurt.

Any visitor encountering the village might describe it as being "dead" at that hour of soporific midges and stupefied flies. It was the wrong assumption. For a man taking guidance from a supernatural entity, whose wisdom is taken as read, Delvin was a bundle of confusion, wondering if he should polish his shoes and shed the attention-drawing dog collar. As always he did neither.

Keen Kev also had the feeling the natural order was going tits up.

This wasn't about him being relegated to batting number eleven. And neither did it count that Margie had her man on a leash. At 'Bramble Cottage' Keen Kev was full of admiration for that. What a woman! he thought, as he often did. No, on this occasion he had simply lost out to Mel, and because of it he had worked himself into a tizz.

His sales pitch for a nice maintenance-free conservatory at the 'Olde Bakery' had included "solid footings, double glazed windows, door and finial". Even so Gerald and Jean had, after much hum and ha, plumped to spend the sizable chunk of their retirement money on fussy wrought iron gates. Something to "make the house stand out". More fool them. "Christmas card Christians," he dismissed them as only showing their faces at the church Midnight, just like the rest of the godless majority – a suitable flock for the troublesome vicar.

Mel's gates would rust in months. Course they would stand out. And for want of watching cricket the unnatural woman couldn't even be bothered to make the things, anyway. The forge was clinker cold. What was today? Tuesday? A normal working day, and she and her annoying mates were at the seaside enjoying the third day of Somerset's championship match. And how they had bragged.

Replete with cold luncheon meat and an overripe tomato Keen Kev played his own game. Hedge-hidden in his back garden nobody could see to criticise. His upended wheelbarrow acting as a backstop-cum-wicket, he lobbed an India rubber ball at the concrete slab that once belonged to the coal bunker, now leaning at just the right angle against the outside privy. With a miniature bat, crudely fashioned from a timber batten, he flicked at the rebound. The ball bobbled away as far as the gooseberry patch. "Four! Great shot by Furet!"

Encouraged, he collected and lobbed again. This time he edged over the hollyhocks and through an irritating hedge gap into Church Lane. "Drat and blast."

An initial recovery attempt on hands and knees failed. The ball was visible, but just out of reach. His scalp protected by his flat cap he scrabbled with greater gusto until his head and shoulders emerged on the far side of the prickly obstacle. He quickly reversed them.

Hurrying from the church, looking furtively this way then that, came Delvin. There was a sound of a car and without warning the vicar darted from view. "I know where you've gone. What are you up to?" Keen Kev pondered. Nosiness itched. After a vigorous wriggle and bleeding from several scratches he was in a position to skulk for the good of the parish. He chucked the recovered ball back over the hedge into a flowerbed before turning his attention to better purpose. Perhaps, a squirrel tailing was due – hypothetically, of course.

He sucked a thorn from his thumb while keeping to the side of the grassy track where he had seen Delvin go. The sun and shadow dappled silver birch and bracken fern, and Keen Kev was careful that his feet avoided the dry snap of twigs and the trampling of purple knapweed.

Where the trees and track petered out to stinging nettles was a stone barn. He heard a voice. "Oh, light of my life, you poor old thing." It was Delvin. Keen Kev inched forward holding his breath and lay doggo, catching a glimpse that gobsmacked. The vicar was groping someone. Whoever it was had their coat collar turned up and wore a brown fedora. Inconvenient ferns, though, obscured Keen Kev's view of whose face it was.

He craned his neck and lost balance. A stick cracked. Alarmed, a cock pheasant rose loud and clattering a yard away from his nose. His cap, fallen over his eyes, almost blinded. He stayed stock-still, biting hard on his top lip.

Delvin stared flintily for what seemed an eternity. "It's just a daft fezzie. Probably startled by a deer. No harm done." He spoke soothingly, and quickly ushered his companion out of sight behind the Wimble-Clatt's stone barn.

Berating himself, Keen Kev decided that to follow was too risky. Best he went home and simply noted his 'ammunition'. The alternative was a stake out to get to the bottom of things. How thrilling!

First though he had to find his sewing kit. A piece of thread was necessary to loop like a lasso. A tick that had warmly secreted itself needed tugging from his torso. Sleuthing from the undergrowth, he discovered, bore hazards.

❖ ❖ ❖

"Blimey, compared to the Bumpkin this place is rough," observed Big Doug, taking in the surroundings of a shabby, art deco abomination.

Griffin supped a cider and gurned. "Rough as the Bay of Biscay. Here, though, we swim with the sordid. Well chosen, Barri boy."

"Griff, you don't half talk some crap. But I'm happy enough," commented Barri. "This pub's got history. Remember Mickie Most, the Animals and Herman's Hermits' record producer? He discovered Racey in this bar."

"Who?" Big Doug frowned.

"Come on! 'Baby It's You'?" Barri beat a rhythm on the table and warbled, "I was lost and at an end. Seems so long, I only needed a friend …"

"Ah," said Mel, sketching in her art book. "You've got us, mate. But betcha me pig we'll never see the scruffbags win the Championship."

"Careful," chuckled Big Doug. "Remember when Old Willy dispensed with his belt when he was guddled? Knotting his Somerset supporter's tie to keep his trousers up, saying that's how it'd be till Somerset won the title? He's been as good as his word ever since, bless him."

"Old Willy's a star, unlike Keen Kev. What a whinger! Know what? I think we should drop him. Can't bat, can't bowl. Useless. Buys himself new kit, for what? Always has a grand in his back pocket yet just whinges, whinges, whinges. Are we supposed to have pity for him 'cos he grew up an orphan? Old Willy's worth ten of that pillock. First opportunity, out."

Griffin tutted. "He's really got under your skin, hasn't he? What do you want? Perfection?"

"Yep." She began making adjustments to her sketch with a rubber and pencil.

"Well, nobody will witness Somerset win anything if they try doing it in Weston-super-Mud." Big Doug ventured. "Not dissing the cricket festival but without us there'd have been more custom at one of Delvin's evensongs. Good win today, mind. Sadly, no repeats of last year's double hundreds from Rosey and Viv."

"Harsh," said Griffin. "When I was a whippersnapper the scruffbags were getting bowled out for thirty-six and thirty-seven. That was the season Captain Tordoff took leave of skippering Naval ships to skipper the scruffbags."

"Scupper, more like," laughed Barri. "Anyway, I didn't think we'd beat Warwickshire so easy. I like the green and quaint, however, playing sardines in the ropey wood pavilion probably came as a shock to Amiss and Kallicharran. They never fired. Willis was whanging down blanks. And our Dasher's fifty was the top score of the match, yay. To cruise home by nine wickets is a gurt thumping in my book."

"Have a look at mine and tell me, honestly, what you think," said Mel, anxiously handing around a sketch of twin gates for the three men to see.

"That's looks grand, Mel," praised Big Doug. "I like the squiggly bits."

Mel swelled with pleasure. "Ta. They're going to be a faff to make. And the job itself will take an age. But least at the end of it Wellard and I can eat."

"You can both bloody retire," chuckled Barri. "I can imagine the pig in a hammock sipping pina colada."

"Keen Kev's proper pissed off."

"For heavens sake! Ignore him. He knows he's unpopular. But he's not totally bad. Just easily led," advised Griffin, banging his empty glass on the table. "So, who's for a game of Pong in the Grand Pier arcade?"

They all looked at one another. "George!" they roared in unison. And off they headed to enjoy the faddish peeps and purps of two-dimensional table tennis. Below them would be the heads of plodding beach donkeys led by capped men, Mel debated, were Keen Kev lookalikes.

Other than the midges the coast was clear.

For Keen Kev there were tingles of excitement, a stirring even, as to what he might see. A tinderbox of impropriety beckoning, and carrying a tin bucket and a lightweight rucksack slung from a shoulder, he ducked and dived to the stone barn.

"I'll collar you, Reverend Clewes," he murmured and had an afterthought. "Bring back tar and feathering."

Reaching the spot where the pheasant had reared he stopped and listened. Only birdsong. Despite that, he continued cautiously. The barn, though, did seem deserted. He edged around its corner to the front yard where he could see a decrepit, dumped campervan and a derelict, wooden henhouse raised on cast iron wheels. Apart from a pair of magpies there were no signs of life. "Hello, maggot-pies. One for sorrow, two for joy." He chortled coldly. "Where do you say I hide?"

One of the birds replied with a harsh chatter.

The barn entrance was devoid of a door, and the two windows held no glass. Inside, apart from some sheep pens and bales of old straw, the building was empty to the rafters that supported a rusty, corrugated iron roof. As he thought: nowhere to secrete himself there, then.

With the campervan a revolting heap, the clever option was the hen house. Which in truth was his idea when he'd set off. From the outside it looked big enough. He slipped the bolt, tearing a thick spider's web. A wrench of the swollen door meant light flooded on dry bird poo, bits of eggshell and feathers. "Perfect."

Taking an auger out of his rucksack he got to work on a spyhole. That done he drilled another, lower, something practical for a Polaroid lens. He neatly assembled a box of sandwiches, a tin of old fashioned mint humbugs, a flask of tea, and an empty milk bottle to pee in. He had almost brought a torch but, instead, ended up praising himself on realising the foolishness. Any camera flashes would likely give him away in the dark.

Patience, however, was needed. And, to balance work and capture, he allocated the likely hours for a roguish reverend.

Perched on the upturned bucket, camera strapped around the neck, he clasped the squirrel tail. Radio headphones fed him Test Match Special observations of England versus India. Sunny Gavaskar seemed forever stuck to the crease like a white-flannelled barnacle.

Keen Kev had no lesser resolve until he nodded off. The bump and clatter arrival of the hay-loaded Land Rover driven by George almost took him by surprise.

"Drat, missed. I love her not." And that time he had really concentrated although his arm had tired. Sitting cross-legged on a mossy root of an oak Barri was throwing single acorns at a Yaffle's nest hole in an adjacent dead tree. An acorn had gone straight in with his first aim. "I love her," he had carelessly said. Then he had settled to a game. Forty-nine further throws and he had failed to repeat the success. And it wasn't as if he hadn't tried. Perhaps, it had just been beginner's luck because he now sorely doubted his feelings.

He stuffed a load of acorns into his pockets. Later he would aim them at his tea mug placed on Nettlegot's stable yard cobbles. The number he managed to lob in would finally make up his mind. Or, at least, might help do so.

SIX

An Odd Couple

At Lord's come the close of play the following Saturday Sussex had done to the scruffbags what Rookton did to the Belters. Throughout the better part of the final Somerset had played abysmally, stuttering to a total of 207. Richards, as if carrying the burden of the West Country on his shoulders, scored a pensive 44. Only Botham with a belligerent 80 batted with his normal abandon. Ball in hand both he and Garner became neutered by the Sussex openers who accumulated ninety-odd for the first wicket. Despite a mid innings hiccough Sussex whizzed home by five wickets with seven overs to spare.

The Snickworthy notables had meandered to Lord's hopeful, but had returned disconsolate – the Bumpkin crew more woebegone than most. Big Doug blamed the "popping plugs" as the car stopped somewhere lonely, the red light atop Salisbury's spire warning low flyers being a distant point of reference. Happily, Griffin improvised. By the glow of a flickering match he jammed the plugs in place using Mel's soggy hanky.

Bleary-eyed, Barri commented they could have been further delayed had they had several orbits of the moon.

By the following afternoon, amid the cautious optimism of the County Ground cram, the Bumpkin crew's powers of recovery were laudable, despite their need to support one another wigwam fashion. Yes, the cup had gone, but there was still the Sunday league to win. After all it *was* Essex, again, that were the visitors.

George hoped Polly might have turned up, too. A search was to no avail and as the match neared its conclusion he conceded defeat. Scruffbags were on the brink of doing likewise.

"Gosh, look up there," exclaimed George, giving Rupert a nudge. Omitted in favour of the Slocombe of Weston-super-Mud, Skid Marks was on top of the indoor school, prowling up and down the roof, witnessing the last rites.

"Let's hope he hasn't become suicidal," said Rupert, feeling guilty that he ought to be taking his pub-running lark more seriously instead of watching cricket through his fingers.

Out into the middle came the scruffbags' dependable one-day dobber and last hope. Trencherman and local egg chaser Rugger Jennings, more red-faced than ever, made wretched attempts at savagery. His blade, brandished with more threat than substance, delivered ineffectual wounds. Scampered singles were meaningless. Boundaries were imperative. They were not to be had. Essex, mindful of their experiences of two weeks before, determined to be stingy. The switched-on gnome, marshalling Essex's field placements like a latter day Napoleon, created an impenetrable screen deploying outfield patrols right into the final over.

"German General, German General," muttered Rupert, his fingers crossed, encouraging the ball to race to the boundary.

"It's Goebbels, not Go-balls," said George, never having before succeeded in dissuading Rupert from inaccurate prayers. "How many times? And Goebbels wasn't a general, he was Hitler's propaganda minister."

"Smart-arse," said Rupert, a comment normally reserved for Griffin.

"Only saying."

In the end four were needed off the last ball. The crowd on tenterhooks, edgy, twitched like a crab in its death throes. Rugger heaved lustily. "Clunk." Defying the law of averages, again he had failed to find the sweet spot. The run chase had come up short and Essex had their revenge.

Submerged amongst fellow supporters massed around the pavilion George, Rupert and the Bumpkin Crew were emotionally drained in a weekend of double disappointment. Neither cared the Quantocks – bathed in evening sunlight – had the scent of coconut wafting from the yellow flowers of gorse. There had been no calypso cricket from Smokey that day. Every scruffbag cup still had a saucer beneath it.

Yesterday Lord's, now this diarrhoea finish. The margin of defeat, two runs. Desperately close. Desperately disappointing. Forty-eight hours ago the scruffbags had been favourites to win both knockout cup and league. Instead, they had become the vanquished. Players braved the viewing box before retreating to hide heads in towels or to simply vanish altogether. Incessant chants expressing absolution and gratitude had overwhelmed, heightening sorrow.

"We made them cry," said Rupert loudly, remarking on the visible tears that had wetted the cheeks of hardy professionals.

Ashen-faced, Nobby the steward brought the crowd tidings from the pavilion. "Last night he hurls his Gillette Cup loser's medal on the Lord's changing room floor, now he's gone and smashed his treasured Stewart Sturridge Jumbo into smithereens in the bathroom."

'Who has?" asked George, overhearing.

"Smokey."

"Viv?"

"Yep, Richards. Innit bleeding obvious?"

Nobby could be excused for not quite being his usual self as he entered retirement. Around him, however, fans continued to cheer and beg for their heroes to re-emerge for one last hurrah. Neither Viv nor any other Somerset player did. But nobody blamed them, least of all George. Back at the spot where he had last seen Polly a fortnight before, he was suffering the blues big time. On three occasions during the afternoon he had tickled Rupert's curiosity by fruitlessly chinning the churchyard wall.

The match result was a secondary disappointment, although George hid the fact, especially from the Bumpkin Crew who, keen to get home to their beds, or in Mel's case to her pig, left him and Rupert to their own devices in the car park.

A trickling tear breached the dam of Rupert's stoicism. Sat in Buttercup, his bright yellow Citroën "deux chevaux" van, he stared at the steering wheel. The van, too, had a dampness that mingled with a strong smell of stale wine – something that Rupert mysteriously blamed on a badger.

Given his friend's silence George began the post-mortem. "After a three hundred and fifty mile round trip to witness a shambles, an empty wallet from drowning despair, and now this. All we needed was a sodding draw. You can't credit it. Two bloody runs shy."

"Just the odd couple," agreed Rupert with a sigh before a rant of wisecracks came fast and mirthless. "What were Beefy and Viv doing exactly? Giving Essex catching practice? Budgie flapped. Perhaps he should stick to playing ping-pong ensconced in his favourite chair. And what sort of name is Slocombe anyway? More porn star than medium pacer and not a maiden bowled. Dredgy almost dug us out of a hole, though."

On the last point George had to agree. "Yep, the Demon of Frome was nearly a ruddy hero. Top score of his life, I bet. But he owed us. The gnome flayed him to all parts of the Shire."

Earlier, things had begun so well. The crowd had rocked on learning that Essex would bat and everything went according to plan. After 29 overs Essex had stumbled to 92 for 4. The previous day was mothballed. Thereafter, came carnage – almost a hundred runs off the final eleven closing overs of mayhem. Scruffbag heads went down, spirits dented. Needing 190 the riposte was poor. With four of their allotted forty over left the West Country men teetered agonisingly on 157 for 7. It was the hope that hurt.

'And yesterday we were just a load of pants," moaned George, which to be fair to him, was not an over-exaggeration.

George pushed the issue. "Why, oh why, after all the brave deeds this season, did we perform so tepidly?"

"Exhaustion, perhaps," Rupert suggested. "It's been a gruelling season."

"Bollocks," retorted George, "We just bottled it. The occasion was too intimidating. We were so worried about losing the game that we were scared shitless to seize the initiative and actually win it."

"Still, fair play to Sussex," said Rupert, "And I'd rather be party to the weekend's debacles than building a stable with my own bare hands like our unfortunate Jerzy."

His emotion at last under control he turned on the van's cassette player. The Wurzels sang about the rivers being "clear and clean in good old Somerset" as Buttercup pulled away, homebound, leaving a few disinterested swans to mosey the Tone undisturbed.

SEVEN

A Badgered Pole

There were few means to escape the village. The charming steam train would puff and whistle tantalisingly near, then bypass one and all. Horses were messy and impractical. Shanks's mare offered possibility to intrepid souls. More so than postulating rigor mortis at the bus stop, where the wooden shelter doubled as a venue for sordid assignations despite the alternatives. With the comings and goings it was logical that the garage remained "open 9 to 6 weekdays". Indelible as the "2/3d per gallon" on the antiquated pump, the hours were underscored on the creaky metal sign of 'Criddle Motors'.

At not quite 6.15 its proprietor perched upon a barstool. Blue overalls smeared in grease and oil, Belters' opening bat Jerzy Bobowski lit a fag, lent back on his bar stool, and blew a smoke ring. He was a true artist, both at keeping cars alive, even after their owners had abandoned hope, and at bolving, whereby he could mimic the sound a red deer stag made during the rutting season, and he did it well enough to get a reply from the real thing. "I'm bloody knackered. Spent all day on the Bumpkin," he yawned, and scratched an itch.

Rupert Shovelton, new to the landlord game, pulled at a pump handle. The ale spat frothily into the glass. "So she's primed ready for tomorrow?"

"Leave out the handbrake turns and she's as ready as she'll ever be. Big Doug and the crew are committed. Well, should be. But I've left binder twine in the glove-box as always, just in case." He took a sip of his pint and grimaced. "Sheeesh, Rupes, you need to change the barrel."

Seeing Rupert's mild alarm at the prospect, Jerzy attempted to steer the conversation into safer water. "Nice ambience, though. Really nice. Old Willy never gave a fiddler's fart. You've made a big difference for the better."

His name in neat fresh white paint above the pub threshold, prematurely balding Rupert, grown pot-bellied by the risks of the wine trade, had taken a further gamble. There was a bohemian edge to the rustic ambience.

Shabby deerstalkers serving as lampshades helped achieve the pub's subtle homeliness. They were the perfect accompaniment to a pair of stag heads. One had the informative plaque "Killed, Dead Woman's Ditch, 1876" and had been won from Sir Robert over a middle of the night game of Black Maria at the rectory. The other, more moth-eaten, had a broken antler and had been on the wall as long as anyone could remember.

Gracing the bar, too, was 'Little Kev'. Occupying a glass cabinet, the stuffed badger dressed in a bespoke yellow check flat cap, yellow check necktie, and matching waistcoat, bared its teeth. Alive, the beast had rumbled out of the rhododendrons to crump into Rupert's van. A dozen boxes of Beaujolais

Nouveau were lost. It had been catastrophic. The precious cargo had clinked all the way from the French vineyard to the last leg of Nettlegot's sparsely gravelled, liberally potholed drive. The badger, Rupert's career changer, indubitably received payback.

Similar could be said of the Snickworthy Players, the local Amateur Dramatic Society, to whom cricket was alien. As a riposte to the pompous clique refusing him an audition for the *Rocky Horror Picture Show* in the village hall Rupert installed his "Empty Heads". Each a parody of a committee member, four redundant cider barrels above the bar each had a gorily painted, porcelain eyeball jammed into its tap-hole.

Rupert ensured his cricket memorabilia had pride of place. Ragged and faded, a maroon Somerset flag with its rampant Wyvern beast, a relic from the 1950s, draped from dowelling tied to an upright bar timber. Framed signed images of Somerset players of the past and signature bats festooned the tobacco tar stained walls.

"Made a change? That's more than I can say for you," Rupert grimaced. "If you go leaving oily marks on that stool you'll be cleaning it yourself, if I don't die choking in the meantime."

"Oh, come off it, Rupes. If it wasn't for my mum and dad here this place would be a bierkeller and you, Rupes, would be wearing lederhosen and embarrassing your knees." Pulling a much-thumbed, slightly blurred sepia photograph from his wallet he flicked away some powdery fag ash about to land on the smiling faces of a fighter pilot sat in a cockpit and a WAAF standing on the wing wielding a spanner over his head. Theirs was a story Jerzy normally told, roaring drunk, to justify not being a total 'furriner', at least less of one than Welsh Barri.

Sobriety helped put life into a semblance of order.

Warsaw was getting a pounding and Tadeus Bobowski was intent on skedaddling. Among the world's best trained, flying scarf snug about his chin, squinting through goggles from his open cockpit, as a pilot of the 'Pursuit Brigade' Tadeus was good, very good.

The amiable Pole and his battered, dumpy, all-metal, gull-wing PZL fighter were a team. About him, however, the Polish Air Force were getting a hiding. Their Luftwaffe counterparts swarmed in planes of higher calibre. The Poles had pluck, but it was bantams versus heavyweights, and really no contest. Many of his escadre had already screamed their Bristol Mercury engines towards impoundment in Romania and Latvia. Opting, instead, for England Tadeus hoped to fight another day.

Fate bounced him down in Somerset with No 2 Polish Fighter Wing in fields on the Blackdown Hills. Hastily requisitioned and with no mains water, Trickey Warren Farm had been rechristened RAF Church Stanton. Farm barns turned into maintenance sheds, control towers imposed themselves, and barrage balloons floated skyward. Libation provided by two pubs made this a liberating place for a Pole. Plentiful saddles of rabbit braised with an abundance of wild mushrooms supplemented wartime rations. In addition, Tadeus was allotted a rationed luxury item – a Hurricane – and he dreamed of a sensible runway.

Oblivious to the war effort rabbits caused chaos. Cook pots aside they multiplied in burrows the size of bomb craters and were everywhere. Sensibly they hopped off an unfinished runway when spinning propellers appeared, except one – an albino without the best of sight. Scrambled and taxiing for take-off Tadeus saw it sunning itself on the warm asphalt. Distracted by the bunny's temerity he bumped into a steamroller with romantic consequences.

Amused, spectating in blue WAAF overalls was pretty Gilly Criddle. Being the daughter of Sam, Snickworthy's master of mechanics on anything from an MG to a Lagonda Rapier, she had picked up wrenches and piston rings from an early age in the garage workshop at the top of the family garden. It was logical the ins and outs of a Rolls-Royce Merlin engine would become second nature. However, making a metal mount for a white rabbit's foot posed a fiddlier challenge after a ruthless flight sergeant dispatched the sunbather by bullet.

Soon Tadeus had the rabbit's foot snug for luck in the pocket of his leather, flying jacket. And there it stayed whether on missions against the menace of the 'Gneisenau' and 'Scharnhorst' or simply having a blast in the skies over Blighty.

At war's end the rabbit's foot had done its job. The politicians, though, had not. Tadeus' homeland fell under the Soviet fist. Disbanded, a triumphant return to a free Poland was out of the question. Like the majority of the one hundred and fifty thousand Polish servicemen under overall British command, he chose a life of exile. He also chose Gilly and a West Country life that, early on, baffled him.

Wanting to eat Bigos, a hunter's stew, him shooting a stag prompted Gilly to slap his wrist and wag her finger, making him promise not to utter a word about it. So ubiquitous rabbit, or, when the garden vegetables were in their prime, plump pigeon, had to do. However, Gilly learned how to make hooch from fruit while she taught him about carburettors and cricket. And it all rubbed off on their son.

And that was how it was until the day the rabbity charm's luck ran out and Tadeus grasped his left arm.

"See how my old mum's pretending to hit my dad," Jerzy said, flashing Rupert the photograph.

"Ah, is that what Margie was doing? Pretending she was going to hit to you? Saw her having a go at you lunchtime as I was passing. What the dickens did you do wrong, now?"

Jerzy quickly changed the subject. "You'll still be selling my apple juice, I hope?" He gave a wink.

Rupert slapped the bar counter. "Course. I've a half demijohn under here. Willy warned me off it. Said it would make me forget the recipe for cheese on toast. Let me have more when you can."

As they both exchanged conspiratorial grins a horse's hooves were heard on the lane outside. They stopped beside a weatherworn, stone-stepped uppin-stock said to have been handy for Judge Jeffries. Alarm erupted on Jerzy's face as a strident female voice shouted, "Stand still, you brute!"

"I'm not here," Jerzy said jumping from his stool. A soft thud at his feet went unnoticed.

"Margie?" Rupert asked. Jerzy nodded. "Okey-dokey," Rupert said. "Probably best if you go hide in the kitchen. When she's gone you can tell me all about it."

The kitchen door had barely shut as a short, plumpish, peroxide blonde tornado pitched into the bar. For her size Margie Mudworth was a formidable force and perceptive with it. She sniffed the air. "Rupert, have you seen Jerzy?" she asked sotto voce, laced with menace.

"Not this evening."

"Oh really? Don't dare lie to me." She pointed a bright red, nail-varnish-tipped digit at an object that lay under the warm seated stool. "That's his disgusting rabbit's foot. Jerzy-Wurzy, come out here now!"

Emerging with a sheepish grin there was evidence of cold roast beef and green salad in his teeth. "I was just ... "

Margie wasn't in the mood for excuses. "As if I don't feed you enough." Her lips barely moved. "There's no use you hiding. If you think you're going to Lord's you can take me London shopping as well. And that's an end to it. Oh, and don't think for one second I'm letting you go to Nottingham. Bondi will need mucking out, feeding and her hay will need collecting." With that she turned on her boot heels.

The sound of hooves vanished into the distance and Rupert looked at his crestfallen friend with commiseration. Worst thing Jerzy could have done was to marry that woman, he thought. He also felt slightly responsible for Jerzy's current plight. However, credit for considerable fine wine consumption had limits.

It wasn't just the delivery van that got badgered.

Rupert sighed. "Um, I suppose this means George and I no longer have a lift in Molly next Saturday," Jerzy's "clever little" Morris Minor Traveler, the mechanic's pride, was a quintessential delight of metal and timber from 1967 – a date every Belter knew as being Somerset's first cup final foray.

Staring unfocused at his ale Jerzy shook his head. He had been doing that a lot recently – what with his mum's arthritis and Margie's demands. The stable grudgingly built with his blood and sweat on the paddock he had struggled to buy off Sir Robert was the tip of the iceberg.

Helping George evict Nettlegot Ned to pasture the other side of the stream to the cricket pitch was painful but not the point. Jerzy felt like his dad must have over Warsaw. However, now it was about the bank balance taking a pounding. Gilly would strangle him if she knew and if she could actually squeeze his neck.

"Well, at least Buttercup'll have more room for the celebratory cider," the fledgling landlord concluded, breaking the silence. At least he hoped it would be celebratory. Somerset's imminent cup final was their first since '67, and there remained just one county never to have won a thing.

If all else failed at least there was another bite at the cherry on the Sunday. That was unless Kent beat Middlesex at Canterbury – complications, complications. A great pity, then, that Jerzy was banned from Nottingham.

Whether the Bumpkin Crew would get anywhere was another question altogether, but not one uppermost in Rupert's mind. That honour lay with the vicar who had become a worrying concern. "Forgot to say," he said. "Devlin definitely isn't going to the final. According to Big Doug he's been ordered to an audience with the bishop?"

"That sounds heavy."

"Fully agree," said Rupert, grimly. "Apparently our Rev's been putting it off for months with his excuses. I know he's up to something. Saw him leap into the bushes in broad daylight as I drove passed the bottom of Church Lane only a few days ago."

"Just so long as he turns the ball sideways against Brockcombe tomorrow and bowls half a dozen tidy overs, I couldn't care less."

EIGHT

Fangless and Stoned

On the last property before leaving the Back Passage the Bumpkin stuck out a nose, idle in its garage – an adapted wartime nissen hut, corrugated curves softened by thick vines of wisteria and the red-tinged leafiness of Virginia creeper.

Beside the nissen was a 1932 Bertram Hutchings caravan that served as storage for wine boxes. A headroom impracticality for Big Doug and inherited from his mum, it was called Angela. With leaded light windows, green paintwork ticked out in yellow, and red wheel hubs, she looked the picture of prettiness. Yet an aluminium shell somehow made her appear as tough as Mel, Big Doug often thought.

The open windows of Wellcombe Cottage let the fresh air into his lungs and helped vent his bass vocal range. "La-la-la-la-laaa." And once more he attempted the high G note required by Shostakovich.

The heavy handbell that lived on the cobbles by his warped, cricket ball red front door, clanged loudly. A dozen or so nesting house sparrows exploded, chittering from the deep ivy growth that clung to the cottage wall. "Doug, you're in the local rag – column inches by that hack Vera Scragg!" It was George avoiding standing on the chewed corpse of a pipistrelle.

Big Doug poked his head out of his music room. "Morning! Mel's already rung. But she was sensible enough to use the phone. And leave Flirty Bertie alone, that tart's in disgrace."

"For catching a bat?"

"No. Looked like Fu Manchu this morning with spaghetti carbonara draped over his snozzle. That present on the doorstep's from paw-batting in the log shed. Don't go touching it, probably piloted by fleas."

Showing its face, a British shorthair happy-go-lucky tomcat rubbed its whiskers on George's jeans, rolled over on its back and spread its legs.

"In the doghouse like his master?"

"Wrong metaphor, George. Tea?" said Big Doug heading for the kitchen.

Bearing the weekly newspaper, George traipsed after him. "You've caused a stink."

Big Doug, on the brink of uttering the obvious, managed to gag himself. "Earl Grey, or 'builder's'?"

"Builders. Pater's gone ballistic, which is ironic. It was you who whomped the ball like a flipping shell."

"That 'lollipop' just happened to ping off the sweet spot. You were at the other end, if I recall. Or were you ogling those girls with a pooch peering over the fence at us from the lane?"

George reddened. "Shut up. Same way their demon bowler with the pink barnet giving me filthy looks seemed familiar, I thought I recognised one of the girls, too. That's all there is to it."

"Yeah, yeah, pull the other one."

"Fact is, the moment I saw her you smashed the church tower's hunky punk."

"I clipped it."

"Uh-uh, and knocked out a fang – at twenty minutes to three going by the church clock." George finally burst into a laugh. "No Belter has ever hit a ball that far. Couldn't tell whether Delvin was rolling in the aisles or crying. You, chap, are the new Gimblett."

"Come off it, George. You can't compare. Gimmo was the cat's pyjamas of scruffbag batsmen. His arms were like tree trunks. That makes him more like Mel. He was prickly as a hedgehog, bottled the emotions of rough cider and was insecure as a dandelion clock."

"And, like you, tonked a cricket ball into a church tower. Good news is Keen Kev actually found the gnasher, bad news is he got the local paparazzi to snap it." He showed the offending newspaper page. "Delvin's considering dangling from the crenellations to stick the thing back on with superglue."

Big Doug spooned loose tea into a pot. "So what does Miss Scragg say?"

"About the Brockcombe game itself, not much. 'Nine wickets for Wardle. Snickworthy skittled for seventeen runs. A six from Birchtree hits a creature chiselled from a mediaeval mason's hellish nightmare.' It's really who she interviewed."

"Let me guess. Keen Kev and Margie's politically correct dadikins, Tristan bloody Mudworth."

"Spot on and I quote: 'Church sidesman Kevin Furet raised local concern regarding the 'costly damage' a cricket ball has caused to Snickworthy church. Parish councillor Tristan Mudworth further commented on the need for the cricket club to provide precautionary boundary nets'..."

"Making Nettlegot look the spitting image of a herring port… Go on."

"'…to protect both an ancient religious building and the general public.'"

"By 'public' he means himself and Margie, I presume. And, where's our demon spinner Delvin in all this, apart from dangling?"

"Dunno. When he sees the bishop it may be raised as an issue, but probably a minor one. Until then he's keeping the fang in a matchbox."

"Milk and sugar?"

"Milk, yes. Khaki colour. No sugar. But listen, there's more. 'Mr Mudworth went on to add that without safeguards the cricket team might have to play future home matches elsewhere, hinting at legal action.'"

Big Doug humphed. "Because a grotesque stone carving – a decrepit gargoyle – might be in need of a denture? Ridiculous. And as we know, there is no 'elsewhere'." Collecting himself he asked George the burning question. "Why didn't you speak to that girl to find out if she was who you thought she was?"

"I told you before. She vanished before I got out. Which meant she could only have been stood there for a few seconds before I lost my off peg."

"Came from being distracted." Big Doug sniffed a potted basil plant on his large sideboard and picked a leaf.

"But as I said, I didn't imagine her."

"Ooooo, the spooks of Nettlegot Manor."

"Piss off."

Digging in the fridge behind bottles of Chardonnay Big Doug emerged with a blob of mozzarella and a slice of Milano salami. The combo magically disappeared. "Did anybody else notice the girls?"

"Apparently not. Which I can believe, given the wonderment of the fang." George swigged his tea and choked.

"Oops, forget the strainer. Well, back to being the barber in 'The Nose'."

Big Doug saw George's bafflement. "Shostakovich. Reliant on the navigation of train drivers and taxis I'm booked for Glyndebourne in a fortnight ... Christ, I must stop mollycoddling that cat. Flirty Bertie, OUT! George, I'm sorry for what's happened, but we need a proper action plan against the forces of ... Mordor."

George replied without hesitation. "Not Mordor, Margie."

NINE

The Sneak Peek

Margie assured him she couldn't care less about the hunky punk. George had just got his knickers in a twist. Whatever her dad was saying had nothing to do with her. Jerzy was so relieved he had actually offered to bring Bondi in for the night.

Clipping a leading rein to the halter was, in theory, a simple exercise well within the scope of his limited horsemanship. After twenty minutes, however, the bolshie nag had reduced him to a state of a gibbering primate. Fractures were detectable in the marital togetherness.

"Can't you put her in?" pleaded Jerzy.

Margie pushed a teetering wheelbarrow of soiled straw toward a pyramidical manure heap that resembled the wonder of Cheops. "Don't know why you make such a fuss about it. The mucking out's done. Only fair you stable Bondi."

"Oh yeah? Fair when it suits you and clashes with my cricket ... For crying out loud!"

The mare had trotted across the paddock, once more putting distance between herself and Jerzy before turning with a look of petulance.

"Imagine you're Beefy. Stick your chest out. Be brave. Show who's boss," Jerzy told himself, determined Margie wouldn't have the satisfaction of his defeat.

"Stay there. Good girl. Stay." Ever so slowly he made another approach until man and horse glared eyeball to eyeball in an exchange of malevolence. "That's it, stay put." To his astonishment Bondi did. Snap. The lead rein attached, he wrapped the trailing end around his wrist, and gave a tug.

Giving a snort Bondi launched. Caught unawares, Jerzy made five long strides and stumbled on a divot. Dragged along, a blur of hooves thudded near his head. Turf and dung spattered him. He lost himself to fear. Last wits let his wrist go limp. The rein freed and he was left lying on his front, shaking like the most timorous of mice. But he was unharmed, apart from a hurt dignity – similar to when he plinked a Keen Kev full toss for a caught and bowled at cricket practice.

"You pillock," Margie scoffed at him, and patted Bondi's withers as the mare nibbled oats from her hand.

She hadn't quite come to grips with being Mrs Bobowski.

Tic-tic-tic. A fixated blue tit pecked at moss and mortar on the window ledge. The bedroom window was open and the noise irritated Margie. Stretching across the dressing table to shoo the bird away her bosom knocked over a tall, expensive bottle of perfume spray. It fell with a clatter amongst a clutter of lipsticks, mascaras, nail varnish, pots of blusher and jars of cleansing lotion. A tub of cotton buds tumbled and spilled on the carpet. She was bending reluctantly to pick them up when the thunderous roar of an engine at full throttle assaulted her eardrums, vibrated glass and drowned out the morning bird song. Her hubby was already at work.

Wedded bliss had waned. An ants' nest and rain clouds were her reward for the pricks and scratches gained in hacking Jerzy and herself a garden sunspot from the brambles and nettles. That topped cooking full English breakfasts, scrubbing Jerzy's oily overalls, and many attempts at ironing the Wimble-Clatt's present of Egyptian cotton sheets creaseless. Not to mention digging carrots at the expense of her nails, plucking a few pheasants, and massacring some rabbit corpses.

What use was it Bondi having a paddock, a stable, and a dented horsebox for the country show when the horse did nothing but munch grass, soil bedding straw, and stare glumly at crows?

That was how it was until Margie and Gilly had a battle of wills.

It was Jerzy's affection that kept her sane. Very different to George, she still considered him an investment. His cricket passion was just about bearable. And their sex life was probably okay. He scored seven out of ten, which was adequate. Only one guy in the village had ever scored the max. Anyway, she was grateful to have escaped the tensions of home, and have a tow hitch on a 'runner'– a beige MOT 'passable'.

Now she had become the one to make the rules.

Still in négligée and panties she leant close to the dressing table mirror and flicked her fingers through her blonde bob. Mousey brown roots were visible. "Maddening." She rootled around on the dressing table and made a mental note to buy hair dye.

"Oooof," Breathing-in and with a wriggle she squeezed into her jodhpurs. Margie sucked in her tummy. Her mummy had once called her fubsy. That was when she wore pigtails tied with blue ribbon. And long before she discovered make-up.

The summer's afternoon many years ago kept smarting the memory. Her eyes had set on the prize, and she began batting eyelashes at George, the boy from the big house. He and Jerzy improvised cricket with a tennis ball. She knew Jerzy. He was at her school. Yet it was the grown-up's bat, a wood-wormed relic too big for George, and the blue set of plastic toy stumps that had her giggling from her bike saddle.

"Stare cat! Stare cat!" shouted Jerzy.

"Ignore her," advised George, grandly. "Bowl."

"Can I play?" she called not meaning it. George played an exaggerated forward defensive.

"No. Go away," both boys agreed in unison.

Margie stayed persistent. "Are you George?"

"GO AWAY!"

"Thaaarp!" She blew them a raspberry. They turned a deaf ear. Chucking her bike down, she stood on one leg. "Look at me, I'm a flamingo."

Jerzy sniggered. "You look more like a duck."

Showing distain, George said nothing. She stuck her thumbs in her ears and waggled her fingers. *He* would notice her. Simple goading, though, proved unsuccessful. Straddling the bike once more, she decided on dragoon pressure. Short legs going like pistons, she peddled up behind the wooden stumps, pulled each one out of the ground, and hurtled off. Although, not far enough away not to notice another boy's arrival. He was older. "Where you been, Rupes?" said Jerzy in welcome.

George finished plonking the stumps back in the ground. "Rupes? Wanna bat?" he asked affably.

Margie had a tantrum.

She was yet to learn fate lay in good fortune and resourcefulness. And good fortune with resourcefulness cantering hot on its heels combined when Margie was a mere eight years old. Ever, indeed, since the teacher's assistant Prudence Biggot, the police constable's wife, flitting around the paint splattered school desk like an irritating sparrow, had upset her during a morning art lesson.

Set the task of painting a picture of an apple tree Margie was the very essence of concentration. Fixed on doing better than fat Mel, tongue sticking out of the corner of her small mouth throughout, she did the best she could with a paintbrush, a jam jar of water and a limited palette of colours. Mrs Biggot, however, was harshly critical. "Looks like broccoli with measles, dear."

Margie's reaction was instant. Excusing herself to the loo she went AWOL exploding out of the primary school gate in a foul temper. Down wind, home was minutes away. She covered it in record time to hear soft moaning drifting from the family bungalow. Her parent's bedroom window was open a small amount and Margie sneaked an inquisitive peek through a gap in the net curtain.

"Mummy! ... I want a pony!" She got one within a fortnight. Although, Tristan, despite dabbling in local politics, remained unsure why, quite out of the blue, Daphne should think it such a necessity. He never contemplated the power of emotional blackmail. Eventually, Bondi, a grey mare, replaced the pony, and so began a love affair.

However, the mystery of who was in her mummy's bed festered. The slurpy sound from under the sheets was 'yuckamuck'.

The problem of stabling was easily solved. Nettlegot provided, just like that. Sir Robert got paid the rent in cash stuffed brown envelopes. Then Rupert Shovelton, the snitch, went and ruined everything. Margie had rued her wasted effort. Whitewashing the cobwebby tack room and giving its window – just about reachable on tiptoe – a lick of gloss had been her naïve attempt at sucking up.

How stupid. The Wimble-Clatts were undeserving absurdities. No, being unable to stand up himself in front of a drunk made George undeserving and absurd – a sissy. Why should she toady? Each rung an obstacle, the social ladder to her proper station in life was slippery. But climb it she would – hook or by crook. A queen bee was what she was. Nettlegot – a honeycomb of corridors, she imagined – merited being her nest. Buzz-buzz. Therefore, although worthier than a lowly drone like Furet, and a rung up from the bungalow, Jerzy was expendable. Which was harsh, she knew. However, he was becoming ever more unpredictable.

It all meant her assets – her tools of guile – were more vital than ever. Of that she was certain. And there was nothing wrong in it. She was a girl and she was foxy. Shameless, she moulted her négligée and considered herself in the mirror. For twenty-five, her boobs were youthful – a smidgen of sag maybe, yet perfectly acceptable. Overall? Not bad.

Grubbing for money she opened a drawer and took out a wooden cigar box hidden underneath her bras. The box's brass clasp resisted her fingernail, but succumbed to tweezers. Inside was a modicum of loose change and a blurry, black-and-white image on thin photographic paper. The latter had been her means of entrapment, effective as a poacher's. Seeing it again made her smile.

Careful to choose the right moment, she had bided her time. Only after the Belters' final game of '78 did she act, and her performance in the darkest corner of the Stump had pleased her. The leading role in the Snickworthy Players was not beyond her capabilities, she felt. Her pathetic whimper, perfection. Her discreet divulgence, pure pathos.

Jerzy had stared dumbly for ages. Him taking so long she had found unnerving. Any fool could see it was an ultrasound of a foetus. Eventually, the enormity of the curve ball fully absorbed, he had gone to the bar and bought himself a double Bushmills. He slugged it down in one. "I'm going to be a dad. Hee-hee." She was incredulous. Not the guilt-laden reaction she had expected and it required a rapid change of stratagem.

"Let's go for a walk," she simpered. "There's a lovely moon." He ordered and knocked back another double.

They strolled arm in arm up Church Lane. Passing a shadowed track where rabbits nibbled Jerzy made a gun from fingers and thumb. "Bang!" He guffawed as the rabbits scarpered.

"You silly," she said.

Under the church lychgate he hugged her. "I'll do the right thing," he said tenderly, "I promise."

From where they stood the lights of Nettlegot shone on the far side of the cricket pitch. "Do you think George will be jealous of us?" she asked.

"Is that so important to you, him being jealous? The Wimble-Clatts haven't always been lords of the bloody manor, you know."

She giggled. "Don't talk rubbish."

"I'm not. Let me show you something. Bet you've never noticed it." Leading the way, he stepped carefully around graves until they came to a large tombstone dedicated to "A veteran of the Battle of Waterloo".

"Take a gander behind that. What do you see? ... Nothing's going to bite you."

She could make out a grave sized grass mound. "It's just a stupid grave."

"That's Snook." He spread his arms out wide in an expansive gesture. "All the land you can see to the lonely hills beyond Nettlegot belonged to the Snook family before a Wimble-Clatt pitched up and nabbed it. There's a reason for the Belters badge having a brown cannonball above the crossed bats."

"A cannonball? I always thought it was a biscuit." She wasn't playing dumb. She really did.

"As for this one, ooo-errgh." Lolling his tongue he imitated a choke with one hand, with his other he jerked an illusory rope above his ear.

"Stop it, you scary man," she giggled. "You're making it up. Nobody's ever called Snook." She threw her arms around his neck. "Snook-snook-snookity-snook." Then she kissed the tip of his nose.

"I'm not making it up. Griffin told me," he said, having reddened. "It's murky stuff. And he sometimes reminds George of it."

"So that makes it true?"

"Well, kinda. And Griffin says Snooks and Wimble-Clatts were related – long ago, of course. Look, Griffin will tell you if I've got the wrong end of the stick, but he's done some rooting around. Turns out, the title of baronet can get claimed by the Snook line – assuming it exists – if the daddy cheese snuffs it from natural causes before any son reaches twenty-one. Some say every Wimble-Clatt needs a good doctor and a good lawyer."

"Whatever you say, Jerzykins."

As they moseyed back it was her turn to yank. Flirtatiously, she dragged Jerzy off the lane and down the track of moonlit shadows until they arrived at an empty stone barn that had a strong smell of sheep.

"This is where I dumped a camper van," whispered Jerzy, nodding to where chrome glinted in a sliver of moon.

"And now you're here again, big boy," She had yawned, stretched voluptuously, jutting her boobs, arousing herself with a fingertip. He pounced. On top of musty hay bales, they coupled, carnal as denizen bunnies. He moaned he loved her. She never uttered a word.

Afterwards, Jerzy smirked oafishly. "Know what I'd like to think? George might be a tad jealous, after all."

So when it came down to it, the grainy image was the reason she was where she was. And to think the portentous scrap had just fluttered from a Filofax and blown her way across the car park as the couple snogged. Initially slow off the mark, she failed to realise the possibilities when she picked it off the ground. However, on the cusp of trotting over the snoggers and handing it back her brainwave happened. She snuck the image into her handbag, concluding the life changer was meant to be.

Jerzy didn't have a clue about babies. He seemed to accept her excuse about the "tragedy of the loo", though, worryingly, he was prone to fiddle with his wedding ring. In fact, he was doing so more than ever. She had to get prepared.

Snapping the clasp shut she returned the box to the drawer. Some money from the garage till would have to go unnoticed. Her hair needed special attention if she was going to London.

At the top of the garden path the engine roared again and then faded into the distance. "Another clapped out heap on a test run," thought Margie aloud.

Downstairs in the kitchen she could hear Gilly's cleaver thwack on the chopping board. It explained the knock on the back door at the crack of dawn. Barri with a rabbit, Margie thought. Exchanged for a couple of pints of Jerzy's scrumpy, no doubt. She wrinkled her nose. Rabbit casserole was not a favourite of hers. The smell of it on the hob permeated the whole cottage.

Now was the opportune moment to go on a cash hunt. After that she would ride Bondi over the tops. And, perhaps, even find Barri playing with acorns while on one of his lonely walks.

TEN

A Sight For Sore Eyes

Joy attacked the newspaper. "I hope you didn't mind me sending George on an errand first thing?"

"Why should I?" Leaning against the French windows Sir Robert continued birdwatching. "I'm sure it was a noble cause."

"Glace cherries, sultanas, and hundreds-and-thousands. Last second decision to make buns. They might bring in a pound or two."

The match flame ignited the squib expertly folded from the offensive page. He smelled the pungent smoke. "Thank you, Joy."

"My pleasure."

Black moustached, a dashing hobby, its plumage dark as slate, closed talons on a dragonfly. Sir Robert admired the spectacle then refocused his binoculars on the church tower. "Birchtree's truly immortalised himself," he mused. "We know not what we do."

The fangless hunky punk was, perhaps, a dilemma solvable by a white elephant. He, though, dreaded far greater hurdles. Boundary nets were an eyesore and their cost prohibitive. Damned if he would kowtow to the whims of Tristan Mudworth.

Berating himself for his own lack of resourcefulness Sir Robert had, instead, put his faith in the Bumpkin Crew by accepting Big Doug's idea to start a fighting fund that was kicking off at that moment.

"When are you planning on going down?"

"To the Bring and Buy? As and when. Thought George would be home by now."

"I wanted to show my face. Maybe even give Lobb a walk." Hopeful, Lobb the Duckdog wagged a tail, whopping it on the threadbare carpet. "But this bloody gout…" The wagging stopped; the dog's look was long-suffering.

As it was the village hall buzzed, more particularly the jam stall manned by Jean of the iron gates. "Damson, quince, and fig, not a shabby choice. More exciting than boring WI strawberry," said Mel, arriving at a trestle table and parking a cardboard box full of kitchy paperback books.

"Nobody's going to be seen dead buying that smut," commented Griffin, grabbing *The Story of O* and scratching the back of his neck.

"Watch and learn."

"You read this stuff?" he asked, adjusting to a perusal of *Fear of Flying*.

"I'm a single woman, I've outgrown *Peter Rabbit*."

"God's sake, put them out of the way for now. I need the space to sort Big Doug's contribution – bin sacks of cast offs from BBC Proms choristers. And he's gone to collect more donated by his other connections, all in his search for atonement."

Mel plonked the box alongside another already under the trestle table. "What's in here?"

"Dunno, haven't got round to looking."

Mel's rummage found a pair of spent Birkenstock sandals, some nondescript children's stories and, submerged beneath several flowery shirts, a brown, felt fedora.

"Who left this?" she asked showing Griffin the hat.

"Haven't got a clue. It was here when I arrived. Barri, maybe. I've not set eyes on him yet. It definitely wasn't George. Earlier I saw him kangarooing the Land Rover. Obviously bound somewhere. My guess, Jerzy's garage."

Trying the hat on for size, Mel gave a twirl of delight on the tips of her 'Doc Martens'. "I'm having it."

"That'll be a quid to the Belters Fund, ta very much." Griffin held out his hand, giving her a glance. "You look like a beachcomber."

"For what? Somerset fossils? Or nits like you?"

"Be nice. Forgot to say, I've got my outboard. It's weedier than I hoped and sounds as tharpy as flatus. Fancy braving a trip in *Pertelote* beyond the lighthouse and an hour of rod-dangling later?"

"Course."

It had been a shortish walk for George. However, the Land Rover had conked out where the only raisable alarm was the "pe-pe-pe" of a meadow pipit. Having returned to the scene he sat patiently on Molly's bonnet.

After sitting where he was for over an hour, George gave a hammy gawp of disbelief. "How funny," he added.

"You feeling all right?" Jerzy held the sooty, dead mouse by its tail. "Trap victim, I'd say." George vigorously nodded agreement. The evidence was fairly clear. "Neck's broken for sure', the mechanic continued. "See how floppy it is?" He gave the pathetic head a forefinger flick. "I'm no forensics expert, but this was dead before it got into the exhaust."

"Thanks very much, Mrs Mudworth. That's an amply steamy one to wallow in," said Mel to the beetling rump. "You're taking all three? Ah, thanks, Mrs Dapling. Enjoy the read. *Virgin Planet* is the *best*. Mrs Biggot, nice to see you. Have a browse. Big change from *Winky the Monkey*."

She turned to Griffin, triumphant. "See?"

"Hiya," puffed Joy, greeting them both. "I've brought you a walnut cake and lemon drizzle, might go down well," she said, taking two tin foil wraps out of a shopping bag. "Really hoped to have had warm buns, but never mind. How's about two pounds each?"

Griffin chuckled. "I'll tell folk they're Nettlegot Manor cakes, and with your reputation I'm sure they'll sell."

"Flatterer," said Joy, cheerily. "Oooh, The *School of Venus*. How exciting."

"What is?" said a voice in her ear.

"Reverend!" exclaimed Joy, "These books are definitely not for you."

Delvin huffed theatrically. "I was actually looking at this scarf." He ran the scarf through his finger and gave a sigh of pleasure. "Cashmere."

"As it's you, one-fifty," said Mel.

He whimpered. "Do you think Jean will take her fig jam back?"

Before Mel could offer opinion Big Doug towered over the table. Delvin made a hasty excuse of having to be somewhere.

"Oh Doug, you've been ages. Seen Barri?" Big Doug shrugged. Mel's eyes flashed. "Let me show you my new hat ... Griffin, seen my hat?"

"You had it under the table."

"Well, now it's gone."

ELEVEN

Operation Squirrel

"For God's sake, Joy, answer the bloody thing! Why doesn't anybody here do what they're supposed to do?"

The ringing telephone echoing around the hallway and down the oak-panelled corridors of Nettlegot brought Joy hastening up from the wine cellar to pick up as commanded. Gout playing up, Sir Robert was in a foul mood made worse by drinking. Immune to the discord, Lobb the Duckdog continued chewing a paw.

It was only five-thirty and, slumped in the red leather armchair with his inflamed foot on a cushioned stool, Sir Robert had already polished off a bottle of Syrah, and he had dispatched Joy off to find another.

"Phew. Hello, Nettlegot Manor," she gasped clamping the receiver between shoulder and ear, freeing her to pick away a cobweb from her dowdy cardigan and check the label on the dusty bottle she held.

"Joy. You sound puffed," said the voice at the end of the line. "It's Rupert Shovelton." Stony silence. "And before you put the phone down, this time it's not about Sir Robert's booze bill. I just want a brief word with George. Please."

Washed by a wave of relief Joy became the essence of cordiality. "Um … last time I looked he was watching 'Shoestring' … I do think Trevor Eve's wonderful. I almost want to move to Bristol … and he's linseeding his Gunn and Moore in the gunroom using some horrible rag. George, this is. Can't see why, with the Belters not having a match at the weekend."

"Ah, and that in mind, I hope he's okayed it for all of us to stay with his Aunt Frances when we're up in the Smoke."

"So I believe. Poor woman."

"You're too harsh. Anyway, I've got an idea to keep George much better occupied than watching a scruffy private eye on the box. It's the reason I rang. Very hush-hush. Just a trivial investment in his time and my piggybank."

Joy winced. "I hope you're not trying to get him started on your grape juices. You'll have me to contend with if you do."

Rupert laughed. "I wouldn't be so bold."

"Hang on, Rupert. I'll go and find him for you."

Doing a quick mental calculation how long that expedition would take, he envisioned himself as Methuselah . "Oh, don't bother. Just ask him to give me a ring back. Thanks, Joy. And there's a couple of small favours I want to ask of you. I'll make it worth your while. Speak about it later. Bye … Oh, and tell him there ain't going be room in the back of Buttercup for any cider." Click.

George returned the call before Rupert could serve Jerzy his first pint of the evening. Before the mechanic had quaffed his second a plot was hatched.

"Listen. Can you use a saw and tape measure?" Rupert whispered down the line.

"Speak up, Rupes. I can't hear you."

"Can't. I don't want to be overheard. Can you use a saw and tape measure?" He spoke as loud as he dared.

"I can make a sheep-proof fence."

"Fantastic. Sounds competent enough. We're going shopping. Whatever else you planned to do tomorrow can wait. I'll pick you up at the bottom of your drive, nine o'clock sharp."

"What's this about?"

"Jerzy. He's sat here now. I'll tell you my brilliant wheeze in the morning. But it's to be kept between you and me. Promise?"

"Promise."

"Wonderful. Then Operation Squirrel is officially underway."

"Operation what? Why *are* you being so mysterious?" For the moment, however, George's questions went unanswered. At Rupert's end the phone was back on the hook.

"You happy staying in Barnes?" asked George, speaking of the posh London suburb, home to Aunt Frances.

"Where better for country mice?" Rupert was in a buoyant mood.

"Certainly preferable to being inside a Land Rover exhaust. To be honest I've never actually met her – Aunt Frances. I know from Pater she got wounded doing something brave in the war. These days, she's always busy running some sort of swanky catering company and is chummy with the Queen of Denmark. She keeps a banger-pooch, and Hobbs and Hammond are free-range tortoises with the run of her marble floors. But I haven't the foggiest where the eight of us are going to be sleeping."

Rupert opened his mouth to say something, but closed it again. As ever his curiosity could wait. With *Sultans of Swing* playing on the tinny radio he leant against Buttercup's bonnet, admiring George at work with a saw. "I'm just thankful we reached the final fair and square. Maybe now we can shuffle Worcester and our Captain Rosey's shortsighted decision under the carpet."

George stepped away from the plywood balanced on the portable saw bench and mopped his brow. "Yep, no more tiddling with slide-rules and making daft declarations." They alluded to an early season cup game in which, after one over Somerset declared their innings against Worcestershire with the scoreboard reading 1 for 0. Although done to ensure Somerset's progress through their zonal group on run-rate, as a public relations exercise it had raised higher hackles than the hound of the Baskervilles.

"Very unsportsmanlike," said Rupert. "Let the dragons in Ivor the Engine's firebox consume the rotter Rosey."

"Just think yourself lucky you weren't actually there," said George. "I was. I mean no, I wasn't. The game was over before Jerzy and I had parked Molly. And we weren't alone."

He remembered most of the hundred spectators paying to enter the Worcester cricket ground had paltry entertainment – namely, the sight of players putting their feet up.

With Jerzy begrudgingly granted leave of absence by Margie the pair had pootled up through the Welsh Marches and lost themselves in the maze of Monmouth. Doing so for nothing had been a waste of Jerzy's liberty.

His gander up, Jerzy told the thin scattering of journalists he had decided on the spot to cease his Somerset membership. Obviously, and much to George's relief, he later changed his mind as he fussed with one of Margie's hairclips under the bonnet in a Ross-on-Wye pub car park – another slight detour whilst on the way home.

However, at Somerset's next home game Jerzy held aloft a homemade banner to greet the scruffbags and their skipper as they stepped out onto the Taunton sward. It read 'IT'S BRIAN ROSE I DO DECLARE!' Unfortunately, spraying the maroon car paint on one of his and Margie's white cotton sheets consigned Jerzy to wifely supervision, and his self-confidence was yanked away like a misshapen nail from a horseshoe.

George flexed his hand before returning to sawing. "Have to agree with you, Rupes. It's not the same without our grubby mechanic. Remember Kent in the quarter-final? Extraordinary. Him jumping up and down and flapping his wings la-la-la-ing the Birdie Song while Budgie Burgess, like a mangel-wurzel turned triffid, scythed away at 'Deadly' Underwood. The Kent collapse was equally remarkable, almost on a par with your nouveau cuisine sandwiches. Griffin's mackerel laced with mustard, apple, and wasp, as I recall." George gave a grimace of disgust at the memory. "Got Jerzy necking warm Cabernet Sauvignon. Urgh. You really do need help in the Stump kitchen, old mate."

"When the right person comes along I'll think about it," said Rupert defensively. "You never know, someone worthy might just tumble out of a hedgerow."

George laughed. "Like our Dasher seems to have done? Maybe he's as big a wonder with a can opener as he is with a bat. I would have loved to see him thrash the Middlesex attack in the semi. Imagine Lord's having to open extra gates for the Somerset fans midweek. Ten thousand without the pressures of silage, barrel changing, and sump leaks, eh?" He sighed at the unfairness of Life. "Anyway, wild horses won't hold me back from Saturday. And Joy's promised me a bulging Tupperware of edible grub."

Deciding to become helpful, Rupert busied himself with a dustpan and brush sweeping up the sawdust from the garage floor, having already stashed precious boxes of vintage in the corner along with his cricket gubbins. "Just think, the scruffbags are probably already gallivanting around the Europa

Hotel in Grosvenor Square."

Obscene luxury, he thought, compared to the accommodation Buttercup offered. He preferred not to dwell on the disparity. "In my opinion Shoestring makes a passable Dasher Denning," he said, uttering the first distracting nonsense that entered his head. "And I take your point. Scruffy garb, shaggy hair, and an off-kilter view of life afford him a clever and deceptive camouflage. Our happy-go-lucky Dasher doesn't exactly come across as your average public school cricket and rugger captain."

"Yep, he's a bog normal village boy at heart," said George's muffled voice. Thump, thump, thump. Kneeling in freed space in the back of the van and using the heel of his hand he persuaded the sheet of plywood into place in a fit of giggles.

Rupert's brow knitted with worry. "Careful, careful, I don't want Buttercup getting scratched. You sure you got the measurements correct?"

"More or less." George found it impossible to be serious.

"More or less isn't good enough. The whole point of this is so that neither of us get claws in our fizzog."

Thump. "There. All done." George rested on his haunches to admire the new partition that separated front from back. "Good, the side windows give enough light. But it's going to get stuffy with them not opening. You sure you've got everything else we need?"

"Affirmative," said Rupert, gesturing a salute. "Beanbag, check. Hamper, check. Magazine, check. Box with ribbon tied by Joy's fair hands, check."

"Wonderful. And more importantly, you sure we're doing the right thing?"

Any hesitancy Rupert might have showed was cursory. "Jerzy will thank us. Although, perhaps not immediately," he said soberly. Then he guffawed. "Better drill a few holes in that plywood. Ensure a bit of airflow."

"And hot breath on our necks. Don't forget to pack earplugs."

Changes complete and the pub locked and bolted by late afternoon they had set off. The warning blackbird went unheard over the sound of the van's cassette player.

"So let the boys all sing and let the boys all shout for tomorrow-oh-oh-ho. La la-la la, la la-la la." The Jam were going *Underground*, Rupert and George were going to a Lord's final singing at the top of their voices. It was the last weekend of the season and the sky was blue. Buttercup purred east along the motorway tailed some way behind by Jerzy and Margie, together with a rabbit's foot that might help speed good fortune.

Set to embark at cockcrow next day the Bumpkin remained to be packed.

TWELVE

A Beastly Bet

A ticket protruded from the breast pocket of Henry Hensher's neutral blazer. Escaping the rat race would have to wait. At least the autumnal nip waned as he queued in the slow moving crocodile of cricket fans.

In front of his nose a couple emanated a small atmospheric cloud.

"I'd love to get my head under the bonnet of one of those red double-decker buses," enthused a West Country burr.

"I'll happily push you under one. You and your stony silences then jabber, jabber, jabber, nothing but engines and cricket."

"I've just bought you your gold bangle."

"So?"

"So why can't you stop whinging for five minutes?"

The couple's bickering was painful to endure. Henry cast around for a distraction. At pavement level a strapping semi-nude towelled himself down. At his feet a kneeling supplicant was about to smack the Adonis in the gonads with a cricket bat in some rite of sadomasochism. A chap in cap and shirt-sleeves held out something that resembled a butt plug. While a bod in plus fours, hands in his greatcoat pockets, seemed worryingly like a flasher. On the fringe minced two cross-dressers. The Roman inspired bas-relief on the perimeter wall of the stateliest home of English cricket, Henry concluded, looked exceedingly dodgy, enough for him to hum *YMCA*.

He felt a tap on his shoulder. "Shut up, old man," whined a voice like a gnat.

Henry half turned. "My apologies," he said catching an egg and bacon striped tie. "Commendable butt plug." He pointed at the detail.

"That's the Ashes urn, old man. You're no cricketer, are you?"

Henry shrugged.

"Why the devil are you here?"

Henry shrugged again keeping shtum, mulling over why someone in his thirties should be deemed an "old man". Gnats live a month, he deduced. The egg and bacon might not see September out.

From habit Henry smoothed his cravat. He had not intended to be where he was. Really, he ought to be home in his bachelor pad making a Plan B. Trouble was brewing. The worst he had known during his decade in the City. Even he, by his own admission not the brightest cabbage in London's stock-broking patch, sensed it. Others much senior were blindly selling stocks as markets tottered. Theirs were acts of recklessness more suitable to penny arcades. Heads would be rolling, most likely his own.

Then over the past week his workplace had been awash with distractions of "oo-aarr-oo-aarrs" and jokes about straw chewing yokels, smocks and scrumpy. Quentin, Henry's friend with a penchant for pints of Northampton Phipps had stoked the fire of rural ambition. Someplace where windfalls and hedge funds had different meanings.

Perhaps carried away by episodes of *The Good Life*, or more likely a strong fancy to Felicity Kendal in a sloppy jumper, impulsively one Sunday afternoon he had bought a copy of *The Complete Book of Self Sufficiency* from a radiant smile and colourful poncho in Brick Lane. The book was pretty much in mint condition other than a noticeable dry bloodstain on a page about making wattle-hurdles, and that he could put up with.

His horticultural efforts were limited to planting a sunflower seed in a plastic pot for a primary school project. His most recent close encounters with the animal kingdom was an alarming Muscovy duck that alighted on his windowsill tray bird feeder. He needed to get reading.

Yesterday, however, during the morning commute Quentin had been clipped off his bike by one of the very red double-deckers that the bus bloke found enamouring. So rather than have a day at Lord's Quentin was enduring a neck-brace and a hospital bed. Cajoled last minute, Henry was assigned to get a full match report of Northants versus "Zum", being told with a sorrowful smile "have a great time, you bastard".

"C'mon Somerset!" The bus bloke's sudden bellow into the lens of a roving television camera made Henry jump.

"Shhh, Jerzy. That's totally unnecessary." Margie admonished, showing the young cameraman both the new bangle on her wrist and a beatific smile.

Biting his tongue Jerzy held back the obvious response about the same being said of over-priced jewellery. "Any sign of George and Rupert?" he asked instead. "That was bloody hilarious, Rupert slipping on the rotten tomato and punting that tortoise. It went like an ice hockey puck across that marble. Gawd, it fair slammed into the wall. Wham! And the dog starts yapping. You see George's face? And then … then Rupert takes the cruddy tortoise to that sink for a clean up and turns the cold tap on, and it goes and hangs out its head from its shell. You say, 'He's enjoying that' and George says, 'If it didn't hang out its head it'd drown.' I was pissing myself. And his Aunt Frances never woke up. Amazing. I'd love to been a fly on the attic wall listening to George and Rupert afterwards. Mind you, they had loads of space up there to avoid one another. It was open season on the camp beds after Bumpkin Crew's no show. Glad you and me got to crash on that big divan."

"For Christ's sake, will you stop wittering? You're getting on my tits."

"Sorry. But it would've been nice to have actually set eyes on George's Aunt Frances. A figment of the imagination, he called her. Going by her morning's notelets we pissed her off. 'Nothing for breakfast. Self cater' and 'Hammond damp and worse for wear. Please, do not touch tortoises. AF.' And both written in finest copperplate."

Margie scowled. "I'll add my finest kick in the balls if you don't quit jabbering. Tortoises are pointless. Reckon George and that idiot must've expired on the tube somewhere. I don't know how I survived. I refuse to be a sardine again. That stink of sweaty armpits – yuckamuck. George has multi-racial competition." She took a tissue from her handbag and wiped her nose. "And look, black smut. I hope they won't show that on the telly. Next time we take a taxi."

"But…"

"Don't 'but' me." The small cloud was threatening to turn cumulonimbus.

"London takes a little getting used to. I took ages to acclimatise." Both Jerzy and Margie swivelled to see who had spoken. Henry grinned pleasantly at them. "Hope you don't mind me butting in?"

Margie did not mind at all. The cloud evaporated. Her beatific smile was flashed again and she immediately instigated introductions.

A cock crowed tardily and gossamer webs shimmered.

"What a catch by Botham!" Griffin clung on to the ball of binder-twine and tumbled to the dewy, thistle rich grass, narrowly missing a hardening cowpat.

"Wow. Can't throw much harder than that," said Mel, admiringly.

The other side of the hedgerow stile Big Doug and Barri continued their confab.

"It was you and Mel telling me to go faster," said Big Doug, indignant. He picked a large blackberry, inspected it for wrigglies, and popped it in his mouth.

Finished ripping away the goosegrass snagged on Bumpkin's wing mirror Barri began picking off fern fronds and pheasant feathers caught on the bumper. "There are A-roads and B-roads and you take us down the smallest bleeding F-road in the county. Admire the grass in the middle. Deserves a mow, this does."

"Did you see any signposts? I certainly didn't." Flapping his arms about Big Doug had reached the nitty-gritty of his frustration. He kicked the floppy tyre. The gash in it was clear to see. "Just hoped to miss the poor fezzie."

"You soft numpty, there's squillions of the pea-brained, suicidal bastards. That pothole was deeper than Cheddar Gorge. Let's just pray you haven't buggered the suspension. As it is we're gonna be really late. I said we should have left earlier. If only we'd gone by the motorway."

Big Doug was unrepentant. "Once you get on there you're stuck."

"And you think we're not stuck now? Are we even out of Somerset?"

"But it's just a flat tyre. All we need is a jack." Helpless, Big Doug uttered the obvious and in doing so made matters worse.

"Duw da! I can't believe it." Barri fumed and warmed to his theme. "Sensibly you get Jerzy to give this heap a once over. Very good. Then, rather than give your house mouse forty-eight hours reprieve, you go and remove the jack from the boot and use it to lift your kitchen sideboard because you want to put poison bait in the mouse hole behind it. Have I got that right?"

"Bumpkin is not a heap."

"Bullshit! Look at it! The gaffer tape over the rust holes isn't even painted a gloss that's close to matching. But that's not the point. My point is, not quite satisfied moving a hundredweight for an ounce you put the effing jack beside the sandwiches and drinks and forget the lot."

"I got distracted. It was my first royalty cheque in ages."

"Bully for you. And exactly what was it for, this cheque?"

"Burping."

"Come again?"

"I burped in Bath Abbey three years ago during a recording of the *Play of Daniel*. It's a solemn piece of mediaeval Latin drama with monophonic music. I was a lion who ate ..."

"Okay, righty-ho. So where, pray, do you plan to find a jack before we starve?"

Look about you, boyo. There's only us four and unremitting countryside as far as the eye can see. Do you even know if we're vaguely going in the right direction?"

"I'm pretty confident we're heading east."

"PRETTY CONFIDENT? Where's the map book?"

"Under the sandwiches."

"Saeson yn arseholes!"

"That's not a nice thing to say about Englishmen, Barri." Mel smiled over the stile. "Lucky I'm a lady or I'd clobber ya. Thought I'd let you happy pair know, Griffin's seen a tractor harvesting spuds and he's running after it. A bit more luck and we'll be rescued. If we're really, really lucky, we might see the second innings."

Barri unfolded a blade of a Swiss army knife. "Reckon I'll start on our road kill. Waste not, want not. No point the flies having it." He was about to trudge the fifty yards back up the lane to collect the pheasant when he stopped and returned to Big Doug.

"Wait a mo. You've got a cat. Cats eat mice. Why even bother with the jack?"

"Flirty Bertie is particular. He's only ever interested in ..." Big Doug began, counted menu items off on his fingers, "tinned tuna ... bats ... and Italian."

"Bonkers. I'm in a world of insanity," said Barri trogging off for the feathered fatality.

Rupert and George, meanwhile, suitably attired in wyvern badged, white pork pie sunhats were already in the ground having each bought their souvenir match programme and scorecard, and had settled, together with a gathering band of Rosey's Army, outside the Taverners' bar soaking up the scene.

Above the pavilion the club flags of Somerset and Northamptonshire drooped in the warm, breathless air. The lush green outfield showed the mower's craft. Ground staff performed last minute preparations with paintbrush and whitewash. A heavy roller trundled up and down. Off the immaculate wicket dust raised by a broom dispersed away down the famous Lord's slope. The head groundsman sneezed and rummaged for a snot-rag. In the stands the morning's broadsheets began to be unfolded and have their crinkles flicked out. In the sports pages there was little about Somerset or Northants. Instead, column inches were given over to Wolverhampton Wanderers paying through the nose for Aston Villa and Scotland striker Andy Gray, setting a new national transfer record of a smidge under a million and a half quid.

A bevy of Northamptonshire players appeared on their team's dressing room balcony.

George noticed the movement, particularly the array of moustaches belonging to Messrs Watts, Larkins, Lamb, Willey, and Sarfraz. "The Mexicans are in the house," he announced.

"Hopefully we can muzzle them from madly firing shots left, right and centre." Rupert snorted.

"Oh, that banner's lovely." George had spotted a gaggle of Somerset fans holding aloft a sheet painted with the words 'BIG BIRD! WILLEY COOK THE LAMBS WITHOUT LARKIN ABOUT?' "Wow, impressive stuff …

"Wahey! Look, look, look, there's Wally of the Willow. He's even worse than Keen Kev." Partly obscured by fetching flower boxes Northants bowler Jim Griffiths peeked over the balcony rail. Of his many ducks, ten had quacked in notable sequence.

Rupert sighed. "Be that as it may, there's still no evidence of the Bumpkin Crew."

The tractor driver, a brawny, curly-haired farm lad, had hastily stopped his spud harvesting. He had seen Griffin windmilling his arms across the field closest to the road and tracked him clambering a gate and jumping into a second where the pats were fresher. Griffin had to cross it to get to the field of potatoes and the idling tractor. The lad was aghast. Leaning out from his cab he put a forefinger to his lips, a clear sign for Griffin to shush.

It did no good. Griffin was standing fifty yards away, the wrong side of the hedge and shouting "help". Cupping both hands to his mouth the lad hollered with all the breath life had granted him. "HUSH YER NOISE! … Oh jeez."

There was a thundering and an excited snort. Out of the corner of his eye Griffin saw something massive – a shaggy, charging blur. Then the air exploded from his lungs and he had a sensation of flying.

Prostrate, winded, and dazed he heard anger. "Hairy Fred, yer bugger!" A meaty grip shook Griffin's shoulder.

"Oww, gerroff." Griffin moaned at a sharp stab of pain.

"You alright, chapper? Nothing broken? That was a gurt wallop he gave yer. He's blind see, but not deaf. He's not a bad sort. Just kinda playful. I'm Billy by the way."

"Griffin. Hi." Griffin stopped watching clouds, sat up with difficulty, and tried to focus on his two new acquaintances.

"Yeah, you're alright." Billy grinned optimistically. "Lucky he just headbutted and didn't horn stick yer. He's a bugger."

"You said."

The bull, Hairy Fred, a long-haired Highland, appeared nonchalant, a vision of innocence.

"Better get that shoulder of yours seen to. What were yer doing running like a mad hare across them fields?"

"Needed help."

Billy chuckled. "Yer need more now after getting Hairy Fred's assistance. Anyway, you were saying."

Griffin explained about the Bumpkin, the flat tyre, not having a jack and about the cricket final. Billy scratched his head. "Yer a bit off beam if yer trying ter get ter London. Never mind, I'll give yer a lift as far as the farm. There's a few jacks lying around there. Cricket yer say? We've got a cricket pitch over in the village. We're not a serious bunch, mind. Me dad still plays. He's the captain. Calls us the Pitchforkers, he does."

"Great stuff," said Griffin. "Perhaps we could give you game sometime."

Had Griffin been in a state to pay full attention he may have detected the sudden glint in Billy's eyes that accompanied his swell of interest. "Yer should speak ter Dad. He'll be in 'The Lion', most like." Billy laughed. "Ken, he's the landlord, renamed it after his cat. Used to be called 'The Rebels'."

"Oh wonderfulness, a pub," thought Griffin. He glanced at his watch. "Your pub got a telly?"

"Not that I know of."

"Surely, if you dad's in the pub and he likes cricket he must be watching the big game today?"

Billy shrugged. Griffin winced in frustration. "Yer need a doctor?" asked Billy, mistaking Griffin's expression for agony.

"Sod the doctor. Help me get that jack."

"Okay, chapper. Whatever yer say. Yer can tell me all about yer team along the way."

As they strolled Griffin did just that. He told about George and Nettlegot, about Rupert and Jerzy, and about the Bumpkin Crew. He chuckled about Big Doug's navigation, Barri slipping into Welsh, and Mel's hothead habit of always betting her pig that she could do anything as well as a bloke.

Billy chuckled, too. "She sounds quite summat."

❖ ❖ ❖

"Can't see Jerzy and Margie, either" said Rupert, fruitlessly scanning faces in the crowd. He had to raise his voice to be heard over a chorus of "Somerset la-la-la". "We need a carrier pigeon to let them know where to find us,"

The scruffbags' balcony remained empty, too. "No sign of Somerset, either." George sounded slightly anxious. "Perhaps, everyone's got lost."

"Trust you to be Mr Optimistic."

"False alarm, there's Rosey ... no he's just disappeared again ... oh, but there's ... what do you think Beefy's quaffing?"

"I've a fair idea." Rupert chuckled.

George had a worrying realisation. "Much good pigeons'll be if the Bumpkin's got trouble and Margie's got Jerzy chained to Oxford Street. Anyway, don't think any of them will find us before the toss seeing as the skippers are strolling out to the middle."

The woes of the Bumpkin and Jerzy were suddenly forgotten. "Fingers-crossed we'll be chasing. It served us well this season."

A flick sent the match coin spinning high before tumbling to settle fates. Captains Rose and Watts stooped, peered, became upright, and shook hands. A BBC microphone and camera shoved in their faces caught the outcome. Those watching the goggle-box across the nation were now better informed than those in the ground. Until Rose, looking towards the pavilion, played a shadow forward defensive. George deciphered. "Gawd, we're bloody batting."

It was clear to every Somerset supporter Northamptonshire had won the toss and Watts had put the scruffbags in even before the PA announcer had cleared his throat. Any dew, though, had by now burnt away leaving conditions that favoured initial use of the pristine wicket.

Rupert was philosophical. "I bet Watts guessed we wanted to chase. But you never know, might be a good toss to lose." It soon seemed it was. Galvanised by the mighty roar that greeted them, Captain Rose and vice-captain Dasher Denning began briskly.

With the score on 34 in the seventh over Jerzy yelled, "That's it, Somerset. Stick yer flag in the field!"

The effect was to have Dasher nick Sarfraz into the gloves of wicketkeeper Sharp. "Go on, amend flag to penance, I dare you" quipped George, before turning his palms red clapping Richards to centre stage, the crowd abuzz.

For George, the moment magic was sabotaged by a violent tug on his arm. "See what I've got," said a familiar voice, turning her wrist so that the bangle dazzled in sunlight. "Oh, and this is Henry. He's a stockbroker, but doesn't want to be. He thinks he wants to live in the country. I said he should move to Snickworthy. I hope you're wearing antiperspirant."

"Hello, Henry," said George. He gave Margie a glower.

"Hi," said Henry, feeling thoroughly awkward.

"Been snared by Margie, have you?" George made a snort. "That's Rupes by the way. I'll be sociable in a mo. Just want to see this first ball to Viv Richards."

Don't be daring today, Smokey, he prayed mentally, *be calm and sensible. Please.*

Happily, there was no disaster. George, puffing out a breath of air that mixed with those from thousands, looked around. "Margie, what have you done with Jerzy?"

"He's getting the drinks in, as if you couldn't guess. I'll murder him for you if he drops the tray."

"There's no need … oh, what a shot! Four!" Richards was away, straight driving to the boundary. Other boundaries followed before Jerzy appeared sloshing pints and putting on a brave face.

Giving George a nudge Rupert mouthed "Operation Squirrel" and gave a clandestine tap of his nose with his forefinger.

"There we go. This'll do lovely," said Billy. "I'll just give it a smidge of grease." He showed Griffin a rusted metal lump. "May need some more from yer Mel's elbow."

Arming Griffin with the precious means of liberty Billy gave directions back to the Bumpkin, and then, importantly to the pub. He had made Griffin repeat them. As Griffin disappeared around the bend of the farm lane Billy headed for the pub himself. He took the short cut going at a gentle stroll across the imperceptible boundary between Wiltshire and Somerset.

The scruffbag skipper was playing patiently when he suffered the death rattle, a stump uprooted by Watts who had scattered fielders and taken personal responsibility. Nine short of a half century Rose walked and Somerset were 95 for two. There was no cause for undue anxiety. At the other end Richards, holding back as George had hoped, was having a gem of an innings. Then came anxiety.

"Golly, Viv's shanked it," said George. The ball looped towards the Taverner's. Two Northants outriders converged. Jerzy cupped hands to his mouth. "Mooo-oooh-aaaah!" he roared. The fielders seemed momentarily thrown into shock. The ball, evading their grasping paws causing a tangle of legs, oofs and ooyahs, bounced safely. And Viv jogged three runs.

Amongst the jeers Rupert laughed. "Let me introduce you, Henry, to Snickworthy's bolving champion." Jerzy was a modesty of smiles.

"Bolving?" The word was alien to Henry's educated vocabulary, so Jerzy explained with a degree of elaboration. He spoke about the tingles in the being of his soul as autumn leaves turned from green to burnished gold, about the breath clouds of stags and the clash of antlers in the chill air in mist-enshrouded combes. Him roaring at dusk was just a bit of fun. "Never won myself a harem of hinds," he sniggered upon finishing his soliloquy.

Henry adopted a scolding tone. "And there was me thinking the word meant 'cheating'." Then his face cracked into a grin. Secretly, inside, he felt the germination of a yearning. However, his attention was drawn back to the cricket when a timed larrup off the sweet spot brought Viv his ton.

"Somerset la-la-la!"

Margie was nonplussed. Rupert, George, and Jerzy, though, had man-hugs. Henry clenched a fist and shouted, "Well done! Come on, Zum!"

Jerzy was amused. "Zum? Where did you come up with that?"

"My friend Quentin, I suppose. It's what he calls Somerset. He's the reason I'm here."

"Zum … hmm … bloody great name."

"Blimey, even that scuffer's clapping!" shouted Rupert. Nearby a policeman in a custodial helmet was having a grand morning.

On 117 the West Indian maestro, incautiously attempting to put his foot on the pedal, inexplicably missed a Wally of the Willow straight one. Groans far outweighed the cheers in the crowd. But they were cheers that were soon pruned.

"I think Watts has damaged himself," Henry observed.

"I think you're spot on, Mr Stockbroker," Rupert agreed. "He's certainly nursing a flipper."

"Looks bad," said Jerzy.

'Yep, he's broken. Rotten luck," said George. "Wonder if he'll be able to bat."

It had seemed fairly innocuous. The routine flat throw from the boundary had fizzed into Watts' mitts. Regulation stuff, normally. Unfortunately, on this occasion for Watts it was not.

His face contorted in pain the captain dragged himself from the field comforted by the crowd's sympathetic applause. Northants were rudderless. Their situation was made worse by the seam-up of Tim Lamb also suffering, prompting amiable jibes about slaughter.

When their inning closed on 269 for eight after the allotted sixty overs the scruffbags were in good shape. Botham coming in at number five had played aggressively. As, by the same token, had Garner.

Between innings Rupert assessed the scoreboard total. "It's competitive at the very least."

"A stroll in the park." said Jerzy, sounding none too convincing.

George voiced the other niggle. "Where in hell's name is the Bumpkin Crew? Are they actually going to miss all the action?"

It was now certain, however, that Captain Watts would. He had suffered a broken bone in his right hand. For him the match was over. Down to bat originally at eight the Northants lower order was now greatly destabilised.

❖ ❖ ❖

Beep, beep, beep. Clunk. Big Doug shoved half the value of his royalty bonanza, a ten pence piece, into the telephone slot.

"Joy? Is that you?"

"Course it's me. There's no need to bellow, Doug."

"We're in Pauncefoot Saint George."

Pregnant silence. "What about George? What's happened?"

"No, no, no. Not our George, England's George... Saint George."

Relieved exhalation. "Are you drunk?"

"Not yet I'm not. Griffin says 'pauncefoot' means pot-bellied. The dragon was obviously no Smaug."

"What on earth are you on about."

"As I said, we're in Pauncefoot Saint George. It's a village somewhere in East Somerset. Maybe Wiltshire. Not quite sure."

"Somerset? Wiltshire? I thought you were at Lord's."

"We were, but the Bumpkin hit…"

"Oh lor."

"I just thought if anyone rang you could let them know we're all okay." Beep, beep, beep. "Well, Griffin isn't quite but…" Beeeeep.

Ken the landlord was being most accommodating. He had bartered a pint and a packet of pork scratchings for Barri's "oven–ready" pheasant on the assurance it was lead pellet free, and now he twiddled the circular wire aerial of a small portable black and white television sharing valuable bar space with a snoozing, large ginger cat. Returning to the table Big Doug plonked down beside Griffin who tenderly adjusted a sling made-do from Big Doug's jumper that supported his right arm. He was already on his second pint.

The flickering television decided to snowstorm.

"A bit more to the left, Ken... Bit more," instructed Mel. "That's better... oops."

"Was that Viv or Big Bird bowling?" frowned Barri.

"Tell you what, let's turn on the radio again," said Ken.

"Yer never said yer had a telly," said a rustic burr belonging to a middle-aged fellow in a flat cap under which he appeared bald as a coot.

"Like I said, Radley, you never asked."

"…. He's out! Larkins is out lbw! Just the sort of start Northamptonshire didn't want. A fantastic delivery from Garner." The radio commentator's news brought an almighty roar from the quickly attuned Big Doug.

Barri leapt at the telly and fiddled manically with the aerial. "There, there. Stop!" yelled Mel. "That's it!"

"Somerset la-la-la!"

❖ ❖ ❖

Northants were three for one. Ten runs later they lost a second wicket, again to Garner. Stubby Welshman Richard Williams, whose height appeared to only reach the Big Bird's belly button, sought an extra millisecond of self-preservation. Too far back in his crease he clouted his own wicket.

The Somerset supporters sensed they were witnesses to unfolding history.

Surrounded by a tipsy chorus in high spirits Rupert, however, was not counting the chickens as a batsman with a busy gait emerged down the pavilion steps. "Here comes Lambie, we've somehow got to get him out early."

Somerset failed to do it.

No relation to Tim, Allan Lamb – a mix of confidence, arrogance, enterprise and sheer bloody-mindedness – took the game to the scruffbags. His bullocking bottom hand guided leather to the boundary with disconcerting ease. He barked orders to opener Geoff Cook of "yes" and "no". Quick singles mounted. So did shots of buckle and swash. The fight back became of worrying proportions.

"For gawd's sake, Zum!" Jerzy was thoroughly frustrated. The Northants duo had reached exactly a hundred run partnership. Thirteen more proved unlucky. The vast and fidgety West Country contingent erupted.

"Oh Peter, you beauty!" Jerzy clenched a fist and cuffed the air.

"What a throw! Superb!" exclaimed Henry.

"Thank gawd for that," Rupert breathed.

"Please, can this be over soon?" whinged Margie.

Probably better off disobeying Lamb's order once a knackered Cook had been run out by the accuracy of Roebuck. Perhaps the Somerset man's spectacles and bookish countenance fooled. Whatever the reason, the second run was never on. Thirteen overs had been bowled. With the Northants score on 126 for three the game was back in the balance.

Willey came and went scoring fewer than a half dozen. Lambie, though, continued to prosper. Captain Rose chucked the ball to Viv. Maybe, a touch of variation might work. In he skipped. Lambie eyes lit up at what seemed a full bunger. He gave it the charge. The speed of Viv's arm had deceived. The ball dipped, gripped and fizzed passed the bat edge. Derek Somerset Taylor did the rest. It was the most marvellous stumping.

Rupert began chicken counting. Viv resumed crouching at slip, Budgie nipped Yardley out from the middle-order to expose the vulnerable tail, and the Big Bird was recalled to mop up.

A knot of off key Somerset wags sang the chorus from a number one hit. "I think I'd better knock – knock knock – on wood!"

To the observer the Big Bird may have been singing the words in his head. He bowled Sharp, then Tim Lamb. That left only the Wally of the Willow.

After one hundred and four years without ever having won a trophy, Somerset were on the brink. Jerzy pulled Henry into a huddle with Rupert and George. Margie admired her bangle.

Every scruffbag fielder was on the balls of his toes. Excited. Expectant. The Big Bird flicked a droplet of sweat away from his brow and roared on by every caring West Country soul he tore in to attack the stumps of his prey. The gap between Wally of the Willow's bat and his pads was less of a gate and more like Nettlegot's front door. The cherry flew unerringly.

Lord's went potty. The stands had an outpouring. The field of Somerset dreams was awash. Spectators ran and gambolled. "Somerset la-la-la" and "The Blackbird" would be sung until voices became hoarse.

"Oh my, oh my," uttered Rupert, quite overcome.

"Golly," said George, lost for words.

"Well, strike me sideway and call me stripy," said Jerzy.

"I've had an epiphany," remarked Henry, "I think I'm a Zum supporter."

That brought a laugh from Rupert. "There must be masochism in your dark side."

"So glad you invited me to join you, Margie. What a grand day."

She bobbed a curtsy then threw her arms around Henry's neck and smacked red lipstick on his cheek. She giggled coyly. "Sorry, I couldn't help myself."

Jerzy and George frowned. Rupert interjected. "Six for 29! That's incredible. Garner took six for 29! Can't believe it."

Henry swore under his breath, remembering his promise. "Poor Quentin. I'll have to go and give him the breakdown."

"You're not leaving us now, are you?" asked George.

"Won't hear of it," said Rupert.

"Absolutely not," said Margie, earning another scowl from Jerzy.

Henry seemed to waver. "Well … what are your plans?"

"Get totally rat-arsed," said Jerzy immediately. "There's this little place Rupes found. Oldest wine bar in London."

"You've twisted my arm."

"Blast! So stupid. Breakdown. You said 'breakdown', Henry." Out of the blue George was agitated. "Don't, any of you, move until I've found a pay phone."

Things had got messy.

The Bumpkin Crew was woozy. Radley appeared so, too, while Mel in light mood expressed the quality of Wellard and the delights of porcine husbandry. On the Lord's balcony Captain Rose brandished the Gillette Cup high above his shoulders. Viv and Beefy lit up cigars.

Switching off the telly, Ken was accusatory. "You're all sloshed."

Big Doug disagreed. He felt blissful. "Never thought I'd ever live to shee it. And winning by forty-five runsh. Ashtounding." He burped.

"Busking now, are you?" queried Barri.

The landlord folded his forearms and sighed meaningfully. "I hope you're not thinking of driving anywhere."

"Nottingshum," said Griffin.

"Yep. Ac nid wyf yn pissed," assured Barri.

The door latch clicked. In walked Billy as if he were carrying buckets. "Hello. Alright?" He nodded at them. "Dad?" He gave Radley a shake. "Yer old bugger, I've finished lifting the tatties. Not much blight."

"We won," Radley smiled bleary eyed.

"That's good," said Billy. "'How's yer arm?" he asked, turning to Griffin.

"Bit shore."

"Have yer asked me dad about playing a cricket match?"

"Er …"

Elbows on table, Mel looked up with interest over the collection of empty pint glasses that surrounded her. She was functionally sober, maybe because she was the only one of the Bumpkin Crew with any banknotes. Although to be fair, Radley had bought a disproportionate number of rounds. "What cricket match?" she asked.

Billy spoke before anybody else could answer. "Yer must be Mel. Them glasses all yours? Cor, yer a rum 'un, love, and no mistake. Pretty, too. A pretty blacksmith, now there's progress."

Blushing, Mel could not help but feel flustered. Composing herself as best she could, she repeated her question, overcompensating with sternness.

Griffin's brow furrowed with effort. "Oh, um, Beltersh vershus Pitchforkersh. Billy shays they're crap. Didn't you Billy?"

Billy was non-committal.

The question Mel had for Griffin was simple. "Was this your idea after the bull knocked the sense out of you?"

He nodded. "Maybe, I was a trifle rash."

Radley, though, seemed cheery enough. "We're happy ter play anyone. 'Tis only a game."

"We'd best ask George before we commit," said Big Doug. "He's our team captain."

"The four of ush are his foot soldiers," added Barri.

"Hang on," said Radley with embroidered surprise. He scrutinised Mel as if gauging the spirit of a filly at auction. "Yer play men's cricket?"

"Course."

"That's not natural."

A deeper flush tinged Mel's naturally rosy cheeks. Dangerous bile.

"I'm going to make some coffee," announced Ken. "Anyone want a mug?"

Each of the Bumpkin Crew raised a hand. Cogs evidently turning Radley slowly hefted his, too.

"Girl's can't play cricket," he chortled with mirth that could be described as exaggerated.

"Yes, they can," said Mel, before mumbling something inaudible.

"Pardon? Speak up, me lovely. Didn't quite hear yer."

The red mist descended. "I said, betcha me pig the Belters beat your rubbish team."

"Mel, no," said Big Doug, frantically wanting to be sober.

"Betcha me bull yer don't," said Radley.

Mel looked Radley straight in the eye. "Done," she said.

"Done," said Radley spitting on his hand. Mel shook it.

"Ahhh. Cor, bloody hell." Radley wiggled his fingers attempting to get back feeling.

"For crying out loud. Soft as a fox's brush, both of you," said Barri, not mincing his words. "Honestly Doug, cats do eat mice."

Big Doug made a last desperate attempt at diplomacy. "Mel, we can't commit to this without George's say so."

"Can't we?" Mel dug deep into her jeans pocket and produced a two pence piece. "Call for home advantage," she growled. She flipped the coin, slapping it down with her palm on the back of her free hand.

"Tails," said Radley.

"Good. First blood to the Belters," she said smugly, revealing a head.

"Coffee?" said Ken putting down a tray. "Everything sorted, Radley?" The farmer gave a nod. Ken then went behind the bar and returned with a recent photograph full of cheesy grins and immaculate whites. "The Pitchforkers," he said. "That's me on the far left. That's Radley in the middle, would you believe it? The bloke on his right played for Dorset a few times. And him with the curly hair got a game or two for Wilts. Didn't you, Billy?"

Billy looked smug. Yet there was something else. Griffin could not fathom what.

The anaesthesia of alcohol beginning to wear off, searing discomfort in his shoulder made him grimace. Digesting the drama two words crossed his mind: clever sods. Radley and Billy, he thought, were deserving of the accolade. The biggest sod, however, was Hairy Fred. Griffin felt pity for himself, for Mel, and especially for Wellard. Yeah, there was always the off chance the Pitchforkers wouldn't turn up. That, though, still beggared a question. "Radley, why wasn't your beast roast beef long ago?" Griffin asked.

The farmer did not reply. Instead, he raised his eyebrows at Billy and Ken. Both shook their heads. "Next spring," Radley said, "Let's arrange the match for … first Saturday after Saint George's Day."

It was fuggy. Below road level on the corner of Villiers Street, a cricket ball's whack from the Embankment, candles flickered in the gloomy vault. A cobwebbed model aeroplane hung from a beam and moved ever so slightly from a modicum of air entering through a small open arched window near the ceiling. Wine varieties such as Pinotage and Torraine were stacked in large wire cages along with boggling numbers of others. The shabby walls were masked with an eclectic mix of oil paintings, newspaper front pages and advertisements from bygone eras. Most of the clientele sitting on tawdry chairs at battered tables were undoubtedly bohemian. George was of the mind none had ever dabbled in cricket.

"Delightful, isn't it?" said Rupert self-satisfied, puffing at a fat cigar, and adding to the nicotine pall that wreathed. "Samuel Pepys used to live here. So did Rudyard Kipling. He wrote *The Light That Failed* in the parlour above us."

"More appropriate for down here," quipped Jerzy, shaking the dregs from a bottle of Chardonnay into Margie's glass.

"Matter of fact, it's the story's about a painter that goes blind."

"That sounds fun."

George opted to butt in and change the subject. "Henry, you must come and visit us for a long weekend. We can put you up at Nettlegot and you can get a real taste of the country."

"How kind. I'd really like that." Henry opened his wallet. "My round, I think."

Eagle-eyed, Margie was instantly curious of flat, teardrop shapes stashed in the wallet's front pocket. "What are those plasticky things?"

"These? Plectrums. They're for strumming my guitar."

"How interesting," said Margie.

"Perhaps, we could encourage our virtuoso here into a game of cricket at the start of next season," said Rupert. "You do play cricket, Henry, don't you?"

"Um, I never managed a varsity blue, but I did play for my college. It was a change to having an oar in my hands."

"George, give this man your number," said Rupert.

Margie dived into her handbag. "Here's pen and paper."

"It's okay," said Henry. "I always carry a Moleskine." The next table became rowdy just as George gave him the important details with the help of numbers of fingers.

THIRTEEN

A Ticking Off

A moth-snatching nightjar purred like a lively sewing machine. Homeward bound and with the day growing dimpsey Delvin's thoughtful walk took him passed the Loop. He saw four fresh faces. New blood.

A man and two girls, all in their early twenties he guessed, carried cardboard boxes and plastic bags from a white van bearing signage 'Brockcombe Garden Services' into Number 6. A brindle Staffordshire terrier squashed its nose against the slobbered van window. The council had been slow off the mark. Mrs Timmins with her forty-a-day habit had been cremated last solstice.

A small girl standing in the lane hugged a large, soft toy rabbit. She sucked on one of its threadbare ears.

"Hello, what's your name?" Delvin asked.

The girl let go of the soggy appendage. "Mummy says I mustn't talk to strange grown-ups."

"Your mummy sounds very sensible."

"Has your rabbit got a name?"

She nodded, her lips buttoned.

"Hi," said the more tired looking of the two girls, holding a stack of records and wearing a metal nose stud. "That's Lili. Her rabbit's 'Rabbit'. Original, innit. You a vicar?"

"Hmm-hmm, I think for the time being I am. Are you all moving in?"

"Nah, just me and Lili. She's my daughter. Them two are my best mates." Faced by a couple with alarming, black spiked hair Delvin made a non-committal sort of noise. Then he knotted his brow, certain he'd seen the young man before.

"They're giving me a hand," the mum added. He got a couple of waves from the front door without anything being dropped.

Delvin clocked matching T-shirts. "Ramones fans, hey?" he called across, now staring intently.

"Gabba Gabba Hey," responded the man disappearing quickly into the house with a pair of mammoth sized sound speakers. The girl vanished, too.

Delvin's raised his voice. "Our blacksmith has them blaring at work – The Ramones. Just imagine." He turned back to the mum. "Look, can I do anything to help, Mrs… um?" Delvin looked at her encouragingly.

"Oh, there's no Mrs. Just Miss. I'm Bridey. Bridey Titland. It's very quiet here, innit? I like it when it's quiet. Anyway, nice to meet you, vicar. Gotta move this stuff. Don't want Lili going to sleep in the hedge."

Bridey sneezed. "Bloody hay fever." A singles record slipped from her grasp. The sleeve landed face up on the ground. Helpfully stooping to pick it up Delvin gasped in disbelief. He saw a monochrome photograph of the

Queen. She wore a tiara and jewelled necklace. What shocked him was the safety pin through her lips. He read the text: "God Save The Queen" – "She Ain't No Human Being" – Sex Pistols.

"Does it offend you, vicar … the safety pin? It's a statement about having to keep your gob shut and a lack of freedom of speech. Bloody genius, Jamie Reid – the artist. Borrow it, if you like."

Delvin hesitated. "Well, yes. I think I will. Thank you."

She raised her eyebrows in surprise. "No probs." She smiled. Lili pouted.

Leaving them to their boxes, bags and 'stuff' Delvin didn't think he would be adding to his congregation any time soon. The sudden loud chattering holler of a blackbird subsiding to a few protesting clucks bade farewell to the twilight. A barn owl screeched as if woken.

No sooner home and slopping around his kitchen in his slippers than an outside thud made Delvin switch on the porch light. "Bad Basil," he chided. He lobbed a stick of kindling from the back door pile at a fox whose bottom protruded from the overturned dustbin. He missed and the fox continued to scrabble after congealed casserole.

"My dear Basil, you're getting braver and braver," said Devlin, admiringly. "S'pose I'll leave you to it, then. If you're really hungry there's more inside the rectory."

The fox popped its head out. Vulpine eyes sized Devlin up. A moment later the animal was gobbling more evidence of the vicar's leftovers.

Devlin flicked the fox into darkness. He meant what he said. There was plenty more. A Pyrex of cold casserole that Joy presumed he'd reheat sat on the kitchen table. He lifted the lid and inspected. Urgh. As ever it looked too unappetising to bother with. "Well, Basil boy I hope you don't tire of the diet."

A piece of hardening cheddar left over in the cheese dish sufficed instead to line Delvin's stomach. He took the stopper off the crystal decanter and poured himself a large sherry.

Had Somerset won? Delvin checked his watch and turned on the radio for the late news. A sombre voice talked about IRA bombs and Lord Mountbatten of Burma's love of boats. "Enough of that." Delvin turned the volume down to silence.

"What a mixed day." He sighed and took off his dog collar.

Earlier, the prime suspect had been Timmy Dapling's mum. She had had the motive to have him sent for. The bishop had made him wait, festering with not so much as a cup of tea. The steady 'doom-doom-doom' of the antechamber's grandfather clock broke the ecclesiastical hush – each swing of the pendulum causing him to feel deeper in trouble.

He totted up the potential accusations and imagined pleading for the daring-do of the Scarlet Pimpernel. There was little he could do to defend himself against hearsay. Nobody could really know what went on behind closed doors.

Contorting his fingers and rolling his wrist he began concentrating on his spin bowling action. "What a ball! Skid Marks gets Willey!"

'Do come in," said the bishop imperiously holding open the door. A blithering mass of uncertainty, the vicar of Snickworthy had his audience.

"Very sorry to keep you so long." The bishop's apology discombobulated Delvin further.

"You should be penitent," the bishop admonished.

Delvin decided on honesty. "Oh, I am, I most certainly am. Timmy should have had more protection."

The bishop was genuinely quizzical. "What *are* you blathering about? I sincerely hope it's nothing untoward."

"No, no, I'm talking about Timmy Dapling. I'm aware it was some time ago now. He should have worn one of those new fangled helmets. But the Belters are very short on kit."

"Pardon."

"It was my fault. I thought he could handle himself better than he did. The delivery wasn't that quick. I presume it's what prompted his mother to write to you?"

The bishop shuffled some papers around on his desk. "I haven't the foggiest notion who you mean."

At that point Delvin had truly thought he would need to look for a job in social work. "If this is about the gossip…"

The bishop was quick to hold up a hand to cut short Delvin's flow. Then he placed a neatly typed sheet of paper so that the vicar could read it. An identical one he kept for himself. "Please comment," he said.

The page showed a set of accounts whose total sum barely amounted to the cost of Delvin's weekly shop, if one overlooked the supermarket alcohol.

"The Church provides you with a rectory in which to rest your weary head and a moderate stipend. I expect better," the bishop said. He looked at the clock on the wall and then to a radio carelessly hidden behind a wilting aspidistra.

"Well, must get on," the bishop chivvied. "Send me your ideas and start rattling that collection plate. We can't have our rectory being sold off now, can we?"

Delvin almost asked the state of the game but thought it unwise. Halfway to the door the bishop had one last thing to say. "I have had a letter – a strange affair. Makes a few accusations towards you. For the time being I choose to ignore it. But I advise you to be careful amongst your flock." The bishop waited for the impact of his words to sink in before adding, "Given that you're a member of a cricket team that's recently vandalised a decorative mediaeval stone carving, can I ask if you ever use the church font as a wicket?" The bishop flicked his wrist to simulate the bowling of an off-break. "Tiddly-widdly, hmm?"

"Me personally? The actual font? … No, categorically no." He had then made his brazen exit. Tiddly-widdly – that had narrowed the field.

Delvin knocked back the sherry and poured another. After methodically shuffling a pack of cards he began a game of patience. Tomorrow morning's sermon could be improvised. His tummy rumbled audibly. "Damn!" He had forgotten to turn up the radio volume. It was far too late to ring Keen Kev, probably already in the Land of Nod dreaming of squirrel tails. Knowing the fate of Lord's had to bide until early communion.

Curious of Bridey's single he turned on his record player and put on the A-side. The din appalled him. The song's closing refrain disturbed him more. "No future, no future. No future for me. No future, no future. No future for you."

Outside in the night air a rabbit screamed. Basil was having afters.

FOURTEEN

Tied Up In Notts

Back so late, George was unsurprised to find a note in the hallway propped, as yesterday, against a photograph of a portly dachshund. Although he was up early, annoyingly, Aunt Frances again was not around. The message beside the fruit bowl read: "Am walking Porthos around pond. Eat. Do not touch tortoises. Do not snoop in drawers. Will not accept reverse charge calls. Let yourself out. AF."

The cold breakfast spread left on offer was no-nonsense but generous – apples and prunes, crispbread and gingercake, cheese and ham, hard-boiled eggs, jam and marmalade and, under a domed silver lid, kedgeree. With the Bumpkin Crew not arriving there were oodles to go round.

By lunchtime Margie intended to be saddling Bondi for a brisk ride. "Fill the lungs full of sea air," she thought, "and blow away the London smuts." There was no reason for Jerzy to have the face of a wet blanket. "Aren't you eating?" she enquired, sweeping crumbs and eggshell from the white linen tablecloth onto the floor marble.

"Not hungry," said Jerzy.

"Ah, diddums. Just because you're missing a lickle cwicket match."

"I'd chomp something if I were you." George did not look up as he poured over a road map. "I just hope the Bumpkin gets to Trent Bridge. Assuming Joy heard it right, Pauncefoot Saint George is here, in the middle of nowhere." He stabbed a finger. "Staggering they got so lost."

"Thought they would've touched base, at least," said Rupert.

"Someone must have tried reversing the charges before we got back last night," said George, smudging Aunt Frances' note wiping at a coffee ring. "Has to have been the Bumpkin Crew. I'll try Joy again before we leave."

Rupert noticed Margie give Jerzy a kick under the table and an "elevate yourself" type of gesture with her hands. "Better do it soon."

"I'll do it now. You check Buttercup," said George weightily, excusing himself. Cramming in a last mouthful, Rupert followed.

Glad to see them go Margie drained her china teacup. From the hall Rupert howled an expletive. "Time to saddle up," she said. "Meet you at the car, Jerzy. Just going for a wee."

"There's no rush, is there? Not as if we've got anything vital to do."

Margie was incredulous. "Bondi needs mucking out and a proper feed. We need a bigger field with more grass. And I want to go for a ride."

The emotion sponge within Jerzy could soak and soak. That moment it could soak no more. "All you ever think about is that effing horse ... oh, and crappy gold bangles."

An icy blue chilled Margie's eyes. "And I have to put up with you and stupid cricket. You better have put the bags in the car in two minutes." She scratched back her chair.

Make that twenty once you've put on your war paint, he thought, moodily.

Lugging an unnecessarily large suitcase and a backpack Jerzy found both George and Rupert outside with the van. "Jerzy, you still want to come to Trent Bridge?" asked Rupert, sounding bright and breezy.

"Don't piss about. Course I do. More than ever."

"Then do as I say."

"What?"

"If you want to come with us, do as I say."

"Am I going to live to regret it?"

"Ummm, probably no," said George. "But there's still time to back out." Within hearing distance a toilet flushed. "Not much, though."

When Margie emerged showing off the benefit of hairspray and rouge, eyeliner and lipstick, the die was cast.

"Hiya, you look great, love." Jerzy grinned like the village buffoon. If a rat could be smelled, now was the time for Margie to smell it. "I'm really sorry about what I said at breakfast. It was selfish. Really, really selfish. Just want to say I've got you a present. I saw it in the jeweller's yesterday morning when you were absorbed with those trays of bangles. It's so you. I was going to give it to you when we got home, but having said what I said, I thought I give it to you now to show how sorry I really am. I gave it to George to look after."

"Yes, that's right," said George stepping forward. "I put it in the van for safe keeping. Here, come and see." He opened Buttercup's rear doors. Margie looked.

There was a wicker hamper, a *Horse and Hound,* and a large beanbag on which nestled a small beautifully wrapped box tied with maroon ribbon. She didn't hesitate.

Slam.

The trap had been set, sprung and secured. "See. Easy as a squirrel," said Rupert, ignoring the turbulent thumps.

"Ridiculous. I feel like a naughty schoolboy," said George.

"You and me both, but all in a good cause. Jerzy, you look pale." It was an understatement. "Let's get going. Me and George have got the map. Jerzy you follow us. It's pretty straight forward once we get ourselves out of London. Straight up the M1. I would suggest a pee break and coffee at Watford Gap services, but given the volatile nature of our cargo ..."

Thump, thump, thump.

"Bye, love, see you later!" Jerzy called out, triggering a muffled expletive and a thumping cannonade. "And please don't worry about Bondi. George says Joy will muck out."

They swung by Barnes pond busy with families. Brown paper bags bulged with stale bread for feeding the ducks. George, hopeful of finding a lady of uncertain age and a fat sausage dog, was disappointed. There was no point for further dilly-dallying. The danger of Margie drawing attention to the van was ample reason.

The threat of having them "summonsed" carried through the plywood divide.

"I swear she's a chimaera. Aunt Frances I mean," said George.

"Bit like the County Championship," mused Rupert.

"What do you think she meant by 'don't snoop in drawers'?"

"Haven't the foggiest."

The Sunday morning traffic was light. In tandem Buttercup and Molly made good progress and soon the Thames was a distance behind.

"It's gone peaceful," observed George.

"Certainly has," Rupert agreed in an exaggeratedly hushed tone. "Hopefully, she's found the Merlot in the hamper and is either engrossed in that glossy mag or away with the fairies."

Thump.

They both sniggered.

"Glad we've brought a tranny," said George. "Be terrible not keeping tabs on Kent. Just hope Brearley's bunch are up for it."

"He's a good skipper. He'll ensure Middlesex don't shirk."

"They must win. And if they do, and we do, I'll send them a big 'thank you' card."

"So will Rosey once he's done admiring his reflection in a second cup in two days."

Their timing in leaving London had been perfect. Converging with cars full of Somerset supporters spewing from Watford Gap, Buttercup and Molly joined the convoy north. Somerset pennants flapped from aerials and convivial horns honked.

Having initially cowered behind the steering wheel from the wagging finger in one of Buttercup's rear windows Jerzy began to relax. "Things never turn out as bad you imagine," he told himself. The problem was he was not particularly imaginative.

Resigned to slump comfortably on the beanbag Margie pondered on the unexpected turn of events. The wrapped box had contained a humbug. And for the second day running there was no ride on the Quantocks. She rolled up the *Horse and Hound* and used it to swat a hitchhiking fly imagining it was Jerzy. The lot of them, though, had been in cahoots. She was sure of that. Even Joy. Thick as thieves. "You won't want me as your enemy," she thought. Opening the bottle of wine she swigged from its neck.

Rupert, wary of a rumpus, parked in what seemed like a quiet side street of red-brick terrace houses. As a welcome a mongrel appeared from an alley, cocked its hind leg and peed on Molly's front tyre. A thin black cat glared caustically from behind an over-stuffed bin. A pigeon perched on a gutter cooed. Humanity, though, was absent.

The cannonade recommenced and a small nose pressed itself against a rear window. "Better let her out," suggested George, "Otherwise she's likely to wake the blinking dead."

"Jerzy!" Rupert called out behind. "You do the honours." After a short delay caused by indecision, Jerzy timorously unfastened the rear door.

Her manner glacial as permafrost Margie slipped down into the street and teetered slightly on her heels. "If we are going to this wretched cricket match one of you had better lead on." The mongrel edged close for a sniff of her leg. She aimed a kick. The animal scooted.

"Margie, I ..."

"No, Jerzy. There's no need to say anything."

The three men grimaced at one another. "The ground's this way," Rupert indicated, setting off. "I'm looking forward to seeing it again. They've just renovated the wonderful old pavilion. It used to be so serene. Can't possibly look so untroubled now. And the lovely Aussie-style scoreboard's been ripped down. Some God-awful office block's got plonked in its place. Progress, eh? Anyway, let's hope that this afternoon, Clive Rice, 'Paddles' Hadlee and their clown 'Rags' Randall keep their powder dry."

"My worry's 'Noddy' Bore's bounce," George chipped-in, thinking of the Notts batting bunny, an indomitable left-arm seamer. He yearned desperately for a better mood.

The tense group crossed an open area of landscaped green space, trudged across the bridge over the Trent, and paid to enter the cricket ground just as Captain Rose lost the toss.

"Somerset la-la-la." An unmistakable deep bass bellowed forth from somewhere amongst the season's last day crowd.

"Big Doug!" George's face lit up. "Ruddy brilliant, the Bumpkin Crew!"

Jerzy bobbed up and down on tiptoe. "Can't see him ... yes, I can. Over towards the weird office tower thingy."

Straining his eyes George laughed. "I think the banner behind him is the one from Lord's yesterday ... 'Garner ... Cook ... Lambs ... Larkin about' ... it is! Good on them!"

"Well, come on, then," said Rupert. "Let's go mingle. Have to say, that pavilion doesn't seem too shabby at all. Good job, Notts."

"Have fun." Scathing, Margie detached herself, grimly determined to find someone of authority. Through the smoke of a burger stall she saw the ideal soul. She popped the bangle into the pocket of her jeans, ruffled her hair and, to reveal a tad more cleavage, undid a blouse button.

"Officer, I've been kidnapped."

The policeman was a bit taken aback by the small indignant bottle blonde looking imploringly up at him. "Really madam? Whom by?"

She pointed. "Those three walking over there led by the pot-bellied bald one in the corduroy trousers. They locked me in the back of a van with a copy of the *Horse and Hound*... Two of them did, anyway – the bald one and the one with the transistor radio. That middle one is my husband and he drove our car. I want to make a statement."

"He drove from where, madam?"

"London. They've all been watching cricket."

"Like they appear to be doing now."

"Yes. My husband followed right behind all the way. Well, I think he did. There were also some cars with noisy horns. And I wasn't always looking."

"On account of you reading the *Horse and Hound* while being kidnapped?"

"Yes." At last, Margie thought, she was getting somewhere. The policeman was starting to take matters seriously – and about time, too.

The policeman bent down to Margie's height and twitched his nose. "Have you been drinking?"

She was disappointed with the humbug. "Only a little red wine in the back of the van. It was from the hamper."

"*Horse and Hound,* red wine ... and ... a hamper?" The policeman was, indeed, beginning to look at things in a more serious light. His tone of voice, however, remained even.

"And where exactly are you all from?"

"The South West."

"South West London?"

"No! South West South West!" It was quite a squawk. Margie had finally popped her lid of patience. "Aren't you going to arrest them?"

The officer remained calm and pragmatic. "Madam, if you don't disappear before I count to five, I'm going to give you a caution."

The glacier melted to a huff.

On the other side of the ground there was much excited backslapping and arm punching. Endeavouring to put a brave face on the Wellard issue Mel embellished jolliness and slapped and punched hardest. "I'm relieved we got here," she said. "Saying that, once out of Somerset, the journey was a dream. The Potteries were a dream, weren't they?"

"A scenic detour," winced Griffin. "However, I've always wondered where Port Vale football club was. After that we drove for miles. By pure luck we found a cricket club. 'Let's pull in here,' I said. And what a lovely bunch of helpful guys. Civilised. You'll never believe this – their pavilion had a library. Langwith, I think the place was. Anyway they fed and watered us and gave us a road map." Griffin stopped talking when he saw George staring at his arm. He turned to Mel. "You going to say something?"

Spontaneously she gave Big Doug a bear hug. "You gurt daft noodle. Ain't he a gurt daft noodle, George?"

Big Doug coughed. "Guess what? Hadlee's not playing. Imagine what the members think of that."

As if on cue the members cheered. Captain Rose leaned over his bat despairing of himself, his stumps demolished. "Brian Rose bowled by Kenny Watson for four," boomed the tannoy.

"Blast," said George, his interest in Griffin's patent incapacity put on hold for a while at least. "Who's Watson? Rosey must have been clearly out of sorts."

"Probably the gastric after-effects of last night," said a dishevelled fellow holding up an end of the travelled banner. "Thought at the time 'oo-er'. There we were, loads of us, falling out of our coaches at Watford Gap and who do we find but Rosey and Dasher tucking into fry-ups. Thought they'd be lording it at some swanky London club and wolfing down caviar. Instead, Dasher goes and helps himself to an extra load of bangers."

"Don't reckon he'd think much of our banger," muttered Barri.

"Sssh," hissed Mel.

Barri did not want to be shushed. "Wish we had the bloody sense to have gone by coach."

Out in the middle, Dasher, true to name having eased perilous singles in pads notoriously too big for him, changed diet to his unorthodox 'Chewton chop'. The ball whomped into the boundary boards.

"Somerset la-la-la!"

Suitably geed-on the Chewton Mendip butcher's son attempted the shot again, got in a muddle and the Notts skipper celebrated having clattered timber.

"Dash, he be out to bowl a' Rice," muttered Griffin.

"Tally-ho! You'll be in plenty of time now for the stirrup cup," called out the chatty banner man as Dasher dragged himself back to the hutch.

Just as he did so just Margie decided to join them. Her ears pricked up. "Does Denning ride?"

"Mendip Farmers' Hunt," replied the banner man. "But only once or twice. Hates being reminded of it. Rotten of me to do so, I s'pose. But hey, it was a silly shot."

It was then that Barri twigged the obvious. "Margie? Weren't you supposed to be back home?"

"Oh, as if you're Mr Innocent," she said rattily. "I know you were in on it."

"You alright? You seem a bit … like you've been dragged through a gorse bush. Jerzy, what's your wifey on about? Wedi'r cwbl! You're not meant to be here either. And why are you hiding behind Big Doug?"

"I'm not."

"Bollocks," Barri disagreed, only to see a wide-eyed Rupert mouthing easily interpreted words. "Okay, I get the message. I'll shut up.... Oh, our man from Oddington's off the mark." Roebuck, the new batsman, had clipped the ball away with some self-assurance.

"Great. Bad news is Middlesex are doing us no favours. They've lost four for 23 and Gatting's out for a duck," reported George leaving off listening intently to his radio for a second. "It sounds like Kent are rolling them over. Even if Roebuck hits a bloody hundred it'll be a wasted effort."

"Nil desperandum," said Griffin. "It's still early days."

Hearing that remark Big Doug could not help himself. "Nil desperandum? You're a fine one to talk after the mess you've landed Mel in."

"Me landed her in?" Griffin was indignant.

"I think there's something the Bumpkin Crew might want to tell us about," Rupert suggested.

Barri took another dekko at Margie, then Jerzy. "Rupes, to be fair, I think you should go first. In fact, I insist."

Ruefully and piecemeal matters got divulged.

Roebuck, meantime, proceeded merrily to a top-notch, hassle-free fifty. Around him Richards, Botham and Marks were cool, calm and collected. The scruffbag total became 185. It was defendable, unlike the actions of certain persons from Snickworthy.

"At least Brearley's bunch have recovered thanks to Eddy Barlow," announced George. His head swam. The fate of a pampered pig and a blind, bovine carpet would be down to the early season form of the Belters. But that was nothing compared to the ripples likely to be caused by Jerzy's destiny. "Knickers," thought George in summary.

Tea brought a simple equation to the more immediate state of play.

Kent had to chase down 182 to win the league. If they failed Somerset had to defend a virtually identical score to snatch the trophy. Griffin decided to concentrate on that fact. "Wonder whether Kent's lime is going to effect matters. Could do if things get tight."

"Too right." Emerged from his shell Jerzy was on the same wavelength. "Bizarre, them building the Canterbury ground around a stupid tree." The tree, being where it was in the outfield, meant special local rules. Shots blocked by it counted as a four.

"I'm rooting for Middlesex," quipped Griffin.

"Kent should call themselves 'Limeys'," said George.

Big Doug, who was actually paying attention to what was going on in front of him, roared. "Well done, Beefy!" Somerset had a wicket. Taylor had a catch. Next over the glovesman had another, off the Big Bird this time. Notts were 15 for two.

The banner men chanted. "Here we go. Here we go. Here we go. HERE WE GO!"

It was irresistible. The crews of Bumpkin and Buttercup together with the man from Molly opened their lungs. "SOMERSET LA-LA-LA!"

Feeling left out Margie pulled her knees to her chin and snarled – a ball of fury.

"The prats care more for Wellard than me." And she believed it. She took the bangle from her pocket, shoved it back on her wrist, and did up the button.

George became pensive, but not from any of Margie's doing. "Kent haven't lost a wicket. They're forty odd now."

"Still early days," repeated Griffin more tentatively, especially as Clive Rice was putting bat to ball. In what barely seemed like time enough to down a tray of ciders Notts were almost within a hundred of the Somerset tally.

George suddenly whooped. "Woolmer, Johnson, Tavaré, Ealham – they've all gone … oh my word, so's Asif Iqbal! Kent are … hang on … shhh … 93 for five."

"KENT ARE 93 FOR FIVE!" boomed Big Doug to any Somerset player on the field who might be interested.

The Demon of Frome gave the impression he was. He immediately produced a nip-backer to trap the Notts skipper ell bee. It was the vital break through.

George leapt with delight. Clonk. "Aargh." He had dropped the radio. A doctor might have diagnosed the ensuing static as "death rattle".

"Give it here," Jerzy demanded. He flipped off the radio's back and fiddled with the batteries. He tutted. "Margie, pass me one of your hair clips."

"Bog off."

"Please, Margie, give it to him," pleaded George.

"I'll slap him in the face with a horseshoe, more like."

"I'm begging you. Give him a hair clip." George made beseeching puppy dog eyes.

Margie caved in, and inwardly cursed her hormones.

Wicket. The Demon had himself another ell bee while Jerzy tiddled.

"There. I think that might hold," said Jerzy, handing the radio back to George in a cacophony of Somerset noise.

"You saviour." Things considered, George's praise was unhelpful and met Margie's frustrated groan.

A united one rose from the members.

"Budgie, you star!" bawled Big Doug. A fine tickle had bought an easy Taylor snaffle. Burgess's aging arm had reduced Notts to 91 for 5 and opened the door to their tail.

George hectically turned knobs. "It's all crackly … oh, hang on …"

"Go easy. The tranny's a bit iffy," Jerzy advised. On the field play was between overs.

"… Selvey's had Cowdrey caught at the wicket. I think Kent are six down … sorry, make that seven," George updated. The Bumpkin Crew, Rupert and Jerzy gave a burst of applause. Scruffbag fielders turned quizzical heads. Big Doug told the latest bulletin to Dasher boundary riding only yards from them. Away he jogged to pass on the message of Kentish collapse.

Spirits ascended higher when, without rhyme or reason, Robinson, the Notts opening batter and the innings cement, had a "yes, no, yes, no" moment of hesitation. It proved terminal both for himself and his team.

The waved ribald banner alluding to 'the Lambs' perhaps reminded Captain Rose of the previous day's Richards effect. Viv was given the cherry. The rewards were miserly overs and a wicket – Hemmings the victim.

Notts supporters heckled, Scruffbag supporters roared and none louder than the fellows from Snickworthy. When Beefy bagged last man Mike Bore plumb ell bee Notts had lost seven for 46.

George fussed with the radio glued to his ear as the scruffbags meandered towards the dressing room. "Kent've had it. They're buggered. 126 for nine. Can't believe it."

"Turn it up, George boyo," said Barri impatiently.

"I can't. I've tried. It makes it go all crackly." So a little corner of Trent Bridge held its breath. "Wayne Daniel's bowling to Underwood," said George taking on the responsibility of commentator. "Last ball of the over. Five left after this ... Wow. Oh, wow, wow, wow!"

"What?" grilled the Snickworthy few.

George spluttered. "We're only bloody champions."

"Serious?" Jerzy looked disbelieving.

"Totally."

"I wouldn't have missed this for the world." Immediately, after his euphoria gushed Jerzy squirmed at his tactless error.

The sun began to set.

Big Doug, however, put hands on hips, drew in a deep breath and bellowed at decibels that surprised all witnesses. "SOMERSET LA-LA-LA!"

Led by Captain Rose the scruffbags eventually ambled happily back onto the outfield to lay mitts on the trophy. As Rosey held it aloft for the travelled tumult Beefy cuddled a jeroboam of Moet et Chandon. Holding a half full glass of cider Budgie Burgess, standing apart, gazed into it thoughtfully.

Dusk having fallen Barri pointed out Budgie, alone on the pavilion balcony. He had tied his trusty cricket boots together. These he hung ceremoniously from a flowerpot, his career complete.

The banner men bade "winter well" and went off in search of their coach. "Suppose us lot had better get along, too." Rupert meant it both ways. "I suggest we follow one another with Buttercup in front." He smiled expressively at the Bumpkin Crew. "Where are you parked?"

"Um..." Big Doug shrugged.

"I'm pretty sure I can find it without a problem," Mel assured.

"I want to go home in the Bumpkin," said Margie, creating an awkward silence that was broken by Big Doug.

"That'll create a bit of a squeeze," he said warily.

Margie jutted her chin out at Jerzy. "Well, I refuse to get in the car with him."

"Oh come off it, Margie. Don't ruin the day," said George. "It's not going to happen again."

"I hate you all."

"Look, we're all knackered and we're not going leave you here," sighed Rupert.

Uttering an oath Barri strode up to Margie and faced her nose to nose."Molly. Now!" Speechless, she gave an infinitesimal nod. Barri wound in his neck and confronted Jerzy, giving him a friendly biff. "Grow some balls," he whispered through clenched teeth.

"Yeah, yeah. Preferably the size of your bim-bom clappers," Jerzy retorted, equally as quietly.

"Righto," Rupert barked. "Let's rendezvous in twenty minutes. Easiest place is the station – plenty of helpful signposts directing one there."

"Afterwards, it'll be a long night's drive," said George stating the obvious. "Tomorrow, Barri, I'll pop down to the stables. I want filling in about the 'Pitchforkers' – the nitty-gritty. Cheer up, Mel. I'm sure it'll all be fine. Wellard, I mean."

A couple of last things occurred to him. "Someone remind me to send a 'thank you' card to Mister Brearley and to have a word with Delvin."

Big Doug, though, wasn't concentrating. "Two trophies. Two! What a brilliant weekend." Doing a take on the quirky, long pig-tailed, New Wave singer, Lene Lovich, Big Doug sang as walked. "My lucky number's one. Ee-oo, ee-oo. My lucky number's two. Ee-oo, ee-oo. Ba-boom, ba-boom."

"Ba-boom, indeed." From Margie it could have been interpreted as a threat.

FIFTEEN

After The Gold Rush

Just before midnight the little crocodile with its transports of ecstasy and gloom pulled into the deserted lamp lit car park of Michaelwood services. Griffin called it "the last outpost of Glawster". Here, he asserted roosted England's cleverest parliament of robber rooks. It voted daily to collectively pick the car park bins clean of the edible – stale buns and sandwich crusts, ham fat and burger scraps. Success was achieved by unity. Breakaway parties were dangerous.

"One lot attempted to pick the lock of a Cortina," informed Griffin as he, Barri and Mel jumped for the loos. They were thirty seconds behind Rupert and George. Big Doug adjusted his discomfort. "I'll stay put. Their rookery nook will be harder to see tonight."

"Don't be a prat. They're all fast asleep, heads under wings," said Barri before making his rush.

Big Doug stayed stubborn.

Sitting in Molly, Margie watched as the company of friends left their vehicles. "You're not going anywhere," she said to Jerzy. They were her first words since leaving Nottingham. She toyed with her gold bangle that only yesterday Jerzy had bought in such a rush. It seemed like an age ago.

Jerzy jiggled. "Oh c'mon love, I'm desperate."

"Tie a knot in it and get some more practice." Margie rubbed a smear of gunk off her bangle with a blouse sleeve and then changed the direction of her life. "Our knot's become a mess and I want it cut."

"What d'you mean?"

"The 'D-word', Jerzy, the effing 'D-word'."

"A divorce? But…" He turned to look her in the eye, but she was staring directly into the car's vanity mirror. "On what grounds?"

Inspired by the Bumpkin parked up several bays in front her answer came from wishful thinking. "Irretrievable breakdown."

"Where the hell did you get your gene pool from? Your parents are so normal."

Margie spluttered a laugh at the remark. Her eyes, though, had widened, almost imperceptibly. "Never won yourself a harem of hinds? Well, hardly a surprise," she quipped. "Go and have your wee."

Molly's door slammed. Big Doug jumped. He wound down the Bumpkin's window. "You alright, mate? … No, no, no, no, no. Don't do that!"

Crump.

Jerzy's size-ten boot had made a sizeable dent in Buttercup.

"Ouch," winced Margie. She ruminated, her words articulated in the mirror. "You godsend, Jerzykins. A family tree, what a wonderful thought."

man's change of countenance. "Is your church tower missing anything? Cor, I bust a gut." He gave Polly a glance. She giggled. He twiddled his earring. "I haven't quite perfected my slower delivery. But the distance that man mountain boshed it was phenomenal."

"But you still ended up with nine wickets," said Larry, back on track. "You're *the* Ollie Wardle, aren't you?"

Ollie smiled modestly. "Does a one-legged duck swim round in circles?"

Larry whistled. "Top wicket taker in the Quantock League. Good on you, son. Question is what to do about the dog, whatever it's called?"

"Wedgy," reminded Ollie. "Pol wanted to call him Pythagoras. Didn't you, Pol? 'Cos his head looks like a triangle. But I told her, the only maths he knows is whether he's had one Bonio or two." He laughed. "We settled on Wedgy, which was Bridey's idea, cos he's a Staffy."

"Don't get it," said Larry.

"Show him your wild strawberry, Bridey."

"They're me best fings," she said, going to open a top cupboard. "I keep 'em out of the way 'cos of Lili." She showed Larry a delicately patterned bone china candlestick and tea service. Larry looked interested. "Thems was Mam's. She's passed on. Wedgwood's from the Potteries. That's Staffordshire." She fondled the dog's ear. "Staffy? Wedgwood? Wedgy?"

"Ah," said Larry.

"Can't help being a fruitcake, can you Wedgy?" The Staffy flopped its tail a few times and, deciding the world was safe and pleasant again, curled up for a snooze.

"Look, I haven't cautioned anybody in three years, but on this occasion I have to insist both you and Miss Bowmer sign my notebook." He gave Polly his most winning smile of charm and reassurance. "And in future I advise you to keep your dog well out of sight of Mrs Bobowski."

"You a cricketer, officer?" asked Polly.

"Love the game, miss. But let's just say I'm like John Arlott. Could never play for sticky toffee."

Polly then showed her concern. "That's a nasty limp you've got."

"I'll live, miss." Larry wasn't going to be fool enough to admit being butted by Nettlegot Ned.

The evening was radiant. On a patch of sparse grass a crow pecked a creepy-crawly supper from Bondi's dung. An unflappable robin dallied for its turn and, the stable door half open, Margie noted the redness of its breast. "Move, or a lunatic Belter will be hitting you to the fence."

There was the smell of fresh straw. Bondi's bridle hung from a peg. Saddle and stirrups were dumped on the wooden saddle horse. Dust billowed. Margie's dignity had taken a bruising and her face still prickled. The claustrophobia of being back in her parents' bungalow had made her increasingly tetchy. Fully aware Rupert would be bandying her embarrassment around the village she continued to chunter as she curry combed mud vigorously out of Bondi's tail.

"That vile dog should be put down. Horrible yobs. Should be laws against them. Biggot did nothing. Nothing! And he has the gall to tell me so. What good's a caution? Useless lump of lard."

"Margie!" Keen Kev was calling from the paddock gate.

"Chuffing Nora. What does *he* want?"

"Margie? Margie! I've got something to show you."

Crossly slamming the curry comb on the oats bin she went outside. There he was, the horrid little man, flicking his foul squirrel tail on the gatepost.

"Kev, I've already told you once. I don't need to see anything to do with your windows – no brochures, no samples – until, if ever, I get planning confirmed. My application's only outline. Understand?"

Keen Kev stayed rooted. He doffed his cap, smoothed his hair, and put the cap back on. "It not about windows, Margie. It's about this." He offered her a photograph to look at. "I took it at lunchtime … at the Wimble-Clatt's stone barn."

Margie snatched the photo, humoured Keen Kev by giving it a glance, and promptly became speechless, apart from a single word utterance: "Mummy."

"Hello you two, lovely evening," said Joy cheerfully, applying her bicycle's brakes and scuffing up dust with her plimsolls. The wicker front basket was full of shopping. "The Camel's in the village hall car park if you need anything. I can recommend the leeks … oops, sorry to interrupt." And away she peddled.

"Well," said Keen Kev," I best be getting on. Might still be some Spam and humbugs. You know where I am if you need any help. I mean it, Margie."

She didn't know if she wanted help, nor knew what to do with herself. Certainly, she didn't want to go home to the bungalow. Fiddling with her gold bangle she knew it was far too late to eat humble pie with Jerzy and Gilly. So, instead, having watched Keen Kev head off, she lay on Bondi's straw and stemmed tears over Mummy and Larry Biggot. "Broccoli and measles," she mouthed, sadistically.

However, one step at a time.

SEVENTEEN

A Blubbing of Curlews

The mat had been bat-beaten and the mattress turned. Curtains and sheets had been scrubbed in the sink, hung on the crab apple tree to dry, and were now back whence they came. There was time to relax.

"So here we are. It's Somerset versus the Indian Tourists. It's a beautiful day in Taunton. And it's Furet opening the batting with Rose. Furet to face his first delivery from Kapil Dev, India's greatest fast bowler EVER."

Keen Kev lobbed his India rubber ball at the slab of angled concrete and played the rebound firmly with his batten into the off side veg bed. A pair of cabbage white butterflies did a bunk.

"What a shot! The crowd is on its feet. What a talent Furet is!"

Next ball – a wayward bung – plopped well wide of his wheelbarrow 'wicket'. No point showing the bat. He was being as selective with his shots as he had been with his selection of photos.

The stone barn had been like ... Keen Kev struggled for a suitable description, and settled for his gran's phrase when she found things busy ... "Piccadilly Circus". The evidence was on his kitchen table along with last night's pilchards that he had been too excited to eat. Margie *was* coming.

Chimes from the church clock told him it two o'clock. She was due any minute. He better have a quick tidy – at least put the rest of his grubby photos out of harm's way in the tomato juice cupboard. The one of George was ... leverage. Others, unexpectedly revealing, made him hot, abashed and nervously fascinated. Boobies. No fedora, though. And, saying that, Reverend Clewes hadn't been forthcoming either.

He picked some flowers – corn chamomile, wild marjoram and 'Burning Love' – as a jam jar centerpiece and then fussed about the kitchen wiping pilchard oil from the floor and tea stains from mugs, folding and refolding the tea towel just so, before shoving his cricket clobber and a dirty dishcloth into the vacuum cleaner cupboard.

He spread some old window quotes and half a dozen brochures on the table, then rearranged the flowers. Burning Love was special, his Gran said. Maltese knights brought the seeds of the crimson, cross-shaped flowers home after the crusades. Going outside to the garden, he went to pick more.

By the time Margie pitched up wearing a sweaty, revealing blouse and dusty jodhpurs, the flowers had begun to droop. "How delightful. Weeds," she said. "Hope I haven't kept you waiting, Kev."

"No, no, not at all. As you see, I've been really busy."

Margie tinkled laughter. "Ha ha, Keen Kev always with a grand in his back pocket."

"If that's what folk say, who am I to disagree?" said Keen Kev not meeting her eyes. "Have you thought about my offer?"

"Long and hard. Mum'll be telling people I need my independence. She won't admit I can't I bear to be in the same house as her. Yuckamuck. Daddy's still in the dark. You are a brick. I accept."

"You accept?"

"I mean where else can I go? But it'll be purely platonic, yer?"

"Oh, without doubt, Margie. Absolutely and completely, " he assured, his heart seeming transmuted by angels. "I'd better show you the spare room."

"Aren't you going to say what the rent is? I'm not sure if I can …"

"Don't worry about that. We can talk about it, later. Follow me. Everything's clean."

It was moving day.

In the village where, to use an old Willy dysphemism, "a sodding muddy-want couldn't fart in its wontwiggle" without folk knowing, the bush telegraph relayed the astounding: Margie had moved in with Keen Kev. The latter swaggered around like a cat that had got the clotted cream, and doffed his cap at his 'guest' at every opportunity. The number of times he had straightened that cap in the bar of the Stump and boasted of her "fair beauty" had become nauseating.

Fair to say the hilarity of Margie's tumble had been surpassed. Yet, there remained an undertone of disharmony residual amongst the Belters since the motorway car park fracas. Barri had honestly intended to keep well out of it.

Keen Kev had better behave himself.

Alone, he traced the line of his scar. What was the attraction? The tartan blanket, damp from the grassy tussocks and moss beneath, began to itch his back. Here the elements often tore futilely at the ancient burial mound and standing stone circle. Not today. Today his balls ached. Empathy. George had put Nettlegot Ned to the ewes. A bird flew across his vision. The angle of the sun meant it was around two o'clock and warm enough for adders and lizards to bask.

"Iesu Grist gwaedlyd." He wasn't best impressed with himself. He would have to see her again, even if it meant just returning the blanket. Anyway, he couldn't not see her – Snickworthy wasn't exactly a sprawl to hide incognito, especially not, as it had proved, in the stone barn.

A glint from the hen house had made Barri curious as he waited, having found a cut dahlia on a hay bale. Putting soldier's training to good use he feigned to leave before stealthily doubling back, using the rear of the barn for cover. Once behind the hen house he couldn't quite believe his ears. "Got it! Botham's hundredth Test wicket! It's Gavasker! Wow!"

Barri sidled around to the door bolt and rammed it into place before slapping the door loudly twice with his palm. "Bird-watching, are we Kev? Let me know if Beefy gets a hundred and one. Failing that, I hear one word of gossip and I'll shuffle you off this mortal coil." And with that Barri ambled away, hands in pockets, whistling tunelessly to hide his unease.

"Curloo-oo." The sound was mournful to empathise his mood. What did Keen Kev know? How much ... detail?

He tried to remember the collective word for curlews. Like his self-respect it had escaped him. "A blubbing." That was appropriate – the sort of word George might come up with. He laughed half-heartedly. Better than Griffin and his stupid 'parliament'.

Eyes shut, caressing blades of grass, he thought how similar this was to the *Elenydd*, the Green Desert of Wales. That was pure beauty. Sculpted by God's spoon. Treeless...

"Mam duw!" Propping himself up on an elbow he leaned over the brow of the small hollow of his lust and carefully unsnagged the frilly lingerie panties from the low growing hawthorn. Their small pink ribbon bow was most fetching. They, too, would have to be reunited with the squidgy bum. Had she left them on purpose? A sniff of scent intoxicated. The little vixen.

Weak, he was. Too easily seduced.

She had passion in her, that girl. Truth was, the wild ponies couldn't have held him back from what was soft and lovely and smelled of musk and roses.

How she had moaned. And how he had pumped away like a randy ram.

There would definitely be hell to pay. A blubbing of curlews, indeed. A distance away a tiny blur of striated brown, its crest raised in excitement, jetted upwards to hover with liquid and peppy trilling. "Who's gone and upset you?" he asked the skylark, putting a little laugh in the last word.

He lay back down in the autumn sunshine. Scarifying the cricket pitch could wait, as could chopping-up Sir Robert's winter logs. On the edge of napping he heard the guttural croak of a raven, the augur of carrion. Himself, maybe.

EIGHTEEN
Flat Tomatoes And Lesser Bugs

Henry turned up the volume of flute and acoustic in his headphones. The music – Jethro Tull – transported him to a place of heavy horses and acres wild, where summer moths came suicidal to dancing candle flame and toddy was golden on the mantle.

A bit of mud never hurting anyone was an old chestnut and out in the clarty countryside, Henry read, it was the season for malting barley.

London didn't have seasons. It had events. Henry had added to them. He had sold his flat. Well, as good as. The offer was one only a fool could refuse. But maybe, having listened to Quentin, he was the biggest chump in the city. Maybe Quentin was right. Yesterday's emotional blackmail and blatant prejudice had made Henry's stubbornness wobble towards a slurry pit of pessimism.

Plan B had "more flaws than a Hackney high-rise." It was Quentin's joke and followed on from him calling Henry "a romantic tosspot". The gist was true. Quentin found Henry's rural desires unfathomable.

Especially so after witnessing Henry borrow a fat leek off the West Hampstead weekend market. The attempted cover drive of a cox's pippin baffled an extraordinary shaggy mongrel that was a cross between a retriever and Bassett hound. Quentin observed Henry's curious reaction when the irritated trader growled a leek that size needed a lot of work to grow. "You think veg grows on trees?" he'd bristled. The pippin had to be paid for.

On the subject of cricket Quentin remained unequivocal. "I go and give you a cup final ticket that are like ruddy gold dust and you repay me by wanting absolution for becoming a Zum fan. If I hadn't been flattened by a fricking bus you'd never have had the slightest interest in Zum."

Obviously Quentin wasn't still just sore from his bus lane tumble. The Northants defeat continued to rankle. He refused to accept Henry's excuse of 'fate'. Negativity had oozed into the next subject. Should the opportunity arise to actually play the game Henry was so rusty he'd need a *Torrey Canyon* amount of lubrication. Why be humbled by Zum straw-chewing peasants?

"Wait till you're pushed," had been Quentin's advice.

The brief letter of resignation had lain on the bijou breakfast bar for days, which accounted for the orange juice stain on the white vellum envelope. Hand it in and dinner party inquisitions would doubtless become ever more excruciating.

"Little bugs have lesser bugs upon their backs to bite 'em. And lesser bugs have lesser bugs and so ad infinitum." Henry hadn't bored of the silly verse no matter how many times he repeated it. In the past hour he'd also absorbed how to move rocks – hypothetically, of course. On top of differentiating between brassicas and carrots, and the topics of moveable chicken arks and fodder beet, it was weighty learning.

Henry snipped some cress, stuck a teaspoon into a tub of potato salad and dolloped it onto a wodge of Sainsbury's baguette already piled with hummus and salami slices. He still had a gut feeling he could 'rough it'. But, perhaps, the cosy illustrations in *The Complete Book Of Self Sufficiency* of pig disembowelment and of birds, bees and haycocks didn't show the full picture.

As he chomped he studied the author photograph of his hero who could have been looking at anything ranging from goose slaughter to a spinning wheel demonstration. Out of shot there was probably even a pair of manure-coated wellies. Sunlight reflected off a thinning pate. Sideburns were bushy. He was portrayed sipping an interesting something or other from a glass-handled pint mug while avoiding a glance at the camera through dark rimmed spectacles. Henry switched his gaze away from the 'bible'.

Having already learned height prevented blight he looked out over the imagined tops of his window box outdoor tomatoes to distant Primrose Hill. Of course, a window box would not do. Nor would his modern kitchen-cum-diner. No matter. He'd never craved for Formica.

A patina aged, long oak table, now that was the thing. Somewhere to sit and pod peas, read a fully spread *Daily Telegraph*, ignore the financial pages, and perhaps tear a rabbit from its 'pyjamas', braising its saddle with foraged mushrooms on an Aga on which he would also fry chocolaty brown eggs from his own...

Henry grabbed his 'bible' and turned to the page he wanted.

... Cuckoo Maran hens. He wondered what noise the hens made and whether they needed a hen house with special hatches.

His own appearance worried him. He was fully aware a short back and sides, polished Oxford shoes and tailored suits didn't quite fit the rustic bill. Saying that, he had decided to keep a standard. A cravat did that. It fitted with his comfy casuals on Sunday rambles through the prim ancient tree-lined avenues of Hampstead Heath. However, that wasn't the real thing. It wasn't Somerset as he dreamed it.

Again the cricket chant from that marvellous day returned to go round and round in his brain. "Somerset la-la-la."

He had to decide on one acre with capital or five and cross his fingers and toes. The 'bible' decreed five could support a family of six. But dammit, there was the rub. His parents were cheery in The Chalfonts. Worse, no fanciable girl in his set of friends would be seen dead in a sloppy jumper. It was a real bugbear. The discovery of rural bliss had to be done alone.

Before taking the plunge he needed advice from the horse's mouth rather than from Quentin.

Getting it was easy.

His black Moleskine diary put somewhere very safe – worryingly safe –

cried for attention. The empty bread bin was almost the last place he'd thought to look for it. The very last would have been his old cricket bag stuffed behind the unused futon along with his battered Harrow straw boater. One he had once loved with a passion, the other he had hated.

Now for the umpteenth time since his latest chat with Quentin he flicked through to the scribble written by candlelight. "George Wimbledon Hat, Nettle Gut, Zum." There was a phone number. Really, all he had to do was ring it and he could be on the first train down for that promised "long weekend". He had been telling himself the same thing over and over.

Again he prevaricated. There were lots of other things he could do. He cast around for inspiration and saw the futon. Making furniture was an option. A creative friend of Quentin's was "making a bomb" having left lecturing at some polytechnic to turn her hand to making ladderback chairs with reed seats – trendy reproductions of those seen in a fisherman's croft while digging for Viking relics in the Shetlands. She could have passed for a kindred spirit of someone harvesting Hampstead leeks.

Unfortunately, Henry never did woodwork at school. However, he was hot on Latin verbs and the FT index.

He half thought about strumming his guitar, but the flat's walls were thin and as ever he didn't want to draw attention. Instead, he placed the Moleskine on the 'bible', put on his new Barbour jacket and removed the price tag. There had to be an event on somewhere, perhaps in one of the local wine bars. He could almost hear Quentin cheering.

He slammed the flat's door behind him. A Cambridge college rowing oar, lettered in gold with 'Lent 1969' and the crew names, including 'H. Hensher', slipped lopsided on its wire hanging.

NINETEEN

Wintry Discontent

The fog blanket lifting, a salvo from the Dapling shoot brought the day's first feathered massacre.

Nettlegot had battened down hatches. Seasonal clobber – sets of stumps, a motley array of club kit, the old school easel with its accompanying time-worn, nail-studded scoreboard, and Mel's crafted plates of tin numbers – was shut in away in the billiard room cupboard along with spiders, mouse droppings, and the brittle carcasses of bluebottles.

Snickworthy cricket snoozed fitfully.

Beyond the steel bar gate, in a well-fertilised part acre, numbers of spindly ash and sycamore had found growing space and ivy wound around the trunks of four mature oaks. A robin piped from a blackberry plump that had yielded to the snout. As had rosebay willowherb and nettles. Lopsided in the muddiest patch of churned-up leaf mould was Wellard the pig's corrugated shed. Each day was a piggy snuffle-grunt of happiness.

No longer in tune, worry about the Pitchforkers' game was causing Mel sleepless nights. It wasn't just that. Billy, she couldn't help think, was 'fit'. Fitter, to be fair, than Barri who was prone to leaving her presents of dead wildlife rather like a cat might leave a mole or sparrow on the mat.

Restlessness had made her chuck aside her sheets and eiderdown before the dawn maggots began scoffing, hence the little basket of unblemished ceps at the smithy door. The fungi would be sizzling later in a frying pan of her making. Amid the welter of hammers, chisels, tongs, fullers, swages and punches, and already victims of Mel's pent-up frustration – two bald hen pheasants, their heads dangling – flopped across her anvil.

The smithy niffed of singed feathers alighting on hot coals. Some, instead, clung to Mel's thick navy blue jumper and her leather apron. Others floated in a visible suspension of sunlit dust particles. She puffed these away while plucking vigorously at an iridescent cock, uncaring that she tore the bird's skin. As she ripped she belted the Ramones version of words of a former sixties hit.

"Everybody's heard about the bird, b-b-bird, bird is the word, Ooo-ooo. B-b-b-bird, bird is the word…" She broke into a sob.

Copper beech leaves continued to tumble. Fairy rings thrived on the Belter's outfield where a buzzard tugged a worm from one of a thousand casts, and moles made mountains. The stretched groundsman, however, was occupied by his other pressing chore.

Bizz-ziz-ziz-bub-bub-bub. Barri's chainsaw reverberated. The wood dressed in the orange, yellow and burnished gold of autumn's meld was, as ever, bountiful.

WINTRY DISCONTENT

The vintage Fordson tractor ran relays with log-filled trailer loads as it had done for over three decades. Chimney smoke ridded Nettlegot of its cackling jackdaws. Of these, one trailing soot skittered down the roof and displaced a lug of lead that had clung on for a century. A heavy slate moved. So did another. "Clack, clack," noted the bird.

Below in the kitchen and hoisted above the range George's cricket whites draped from the rack clothes airer. Red and green streaky patches remained discernible, resisting Joy's obdurate scrubbings. She sighed. The flipping stains could stay. She had done her best. Bleach was a no-no. It chapped her hands to rawness. Despite wrangles over the mangle Sir Robert had flatly denied the need for a modern washing machine. Getting hold of fortified wine from Rupert was far weightier. "Any port in a storm will do, my dear chap," the knight weedled, naive to the calamitous tidal change of fortune.

The solstice was cantering ever closer. Beyond lay the Pitchforkers match and George had yet to break the news. There really hadn't been the opportunity. What with the drag of itch mite, blow-fly, ticks and lice, he was too busy for cricketing distractions, and 'slip position' had a whole new connotation. Careful not to drown himself in noxious insecticide and fungicide the ewes were duly dipped.

Not only that, he was also up to his eyeballs with their arses. The scaggy wool around their tails needed clipping, beautifying them for tupping.

In turn, the rugby-tackled wether lambs had to be shoved inside the stone barn for a further fatten. To fill their tums, sugar beets, at least those that survived deer munching, needed harvesting. From the scant crop arose a problem – sheep nuts.

Getting hold of winter stores underscored the red, more indelible than any ball mark on cricket whites, in Sir Robert's accounts.

Topping things off, Jerzy and Rupert had needed consoling. George felt drained. "Blooming heck," he sighed wearily on his papa wanting "a word".

Facing Sir Robert, he fidgeted.

"First things first, and sorry to be blunt, but I'm considering selling Nettlegot Ned," announced the old man.

"The ram? No! Why?"

"Enough!" Ensconced in his favoured armchair Sir Robert pointed the family's ivory handled letter knife at George, waving two letters. One was blessed with delightful handwriting. Who that was from was obvious. Aunt Frances had taken her time. "I want explanations and no beating about the bush. See here ... She's displeased about mess deposited on the floor during breakfast." Sir Robert tapped a particular line of handwriting. "'... encourages the dog to scavenge. Barnes pond provides bother enough.'"

"That *might* have been Margie Bobowski." The palaver was all about crumbs – a minor faux pas. Although it was bad form to tell on someone even if they probably were guilty, internally, his sense of relief grew. It was quickly pruned.

Sir Robert peered closely at his son over the brim of his reading glasses. "Also ... playing curling twice with a tortoise? ... *And*" He tapped the letter again.

"Fudge, here it comes," thought George, doing his best not to swear. He shuffled uneasily.

"The dear old thing claims to have witnessed ... Look at me when I'm talking to you ... a kidnap of a houseguest. Any idea what she's on about?"

George's tongue disappeared into a vortex.

"For goodness sake," said Sir Robert, pressing on the point. "It says here she wants me to read you the Riot Act. Don't stand there like a swede-topped scarecrow. Explain."

"It was Margie Bobowski," mumbled George.

"You've already said that, you ninny. I'm asking you about the kidnap, not the messy floor or tortoise."

The sound that came from George was very small and didn't particularly suit his stature. "The tortoise was Rupes' fault."

"I don't give a fiddler's fart about the tortoise! Who did you ... Saints preserve me ... kidnap?"

George tugged at his shirt, feeling mortifying odour pool in his armpits. "Margie. It was *probably* Margie. But it wasn't a kidnap. It really wasn't. Rupes and I just wanted Jerzy to see the cricket that last Sunday of the season. The Nottingham game."

"And to achieve that you felt the need to bundle Mrs Bobowski kicking and screaming into the back of a van?"

"She wasn't ... and she's so ... well, you know ... " George gave up.

"Have you considered the fall out if Aunt Frances writes chummily about this fiasco to the Queen of Denmark? The name Wimble-Clatt will be dragged through the courts of Europe."

"What is it between you and that Bobowski girl?" Sir Robert seemed genuinely interested.

"It's nothing to do with me. It's all her."

"Refresh my memory. As I recall, had Mr Shovelton and I not pulled you from the tack room once upon a time, your virginity would have jogged off with the devil in a handcart."

"Pater!"

"Happily, she seems none the worse for her confinement. Saw her earlier – the usual sack of spuds on that bally nag ..." Sir Robert seemed to collect himself together. "Point is, George, she's making an application for outline planning permission on that paddock I sold that husband of hers and, quite frankly, I'm wondering if it's anything personal."

George was gobsmacked. "She can't. The paddock's not hers ... I know she and Jerzy are divorcing ... but ... He never said ..." Out in the hallway he heard the phone ring. It was quickly silenced. His gaze travelled from his papa to the view of the cricket pitch out through the window. Audible still was the distant buzz of the chainsaw.

"I've spoken to Gilly at the garage," said Sir Robert. "Seems her son transferred the paddock into his wife's name as soon as he bought the land off me. Gilly was furious about it at the time, her family's money and all that."

"Er, what's Margie want the planning permission for?" Though asking the question George didn't really want to know the answer.

"Bungalows. Bloody bungalows. If she succeeds it'll mean all sorts of wretched strangers arriving in Snickworthy. Which brings me to this other matter." Sir Robert shook the second missive.

George caught a glance of the letterhead. "The Lion Inn, Pauncefoot Saint George."

He reeled.

The door opened with a knock. "Only me," said Joy, holding a duster and a can of polish. "Everything alright? There was a call for you, George. I said you were busy. But I said you'd call him back. Somebody called Henry Hensher."

Margie was in fine fettle.

Flumped across Bondi's saddle she listened to the chainsaw. "Naughty boy."

Need she expose the selfish and irresponsible wild tryst? Perhaps. It was a gift-horse and she knew she was jealous.

For her part she had been beavering. Armed with a genealogist's bumph she had scoured post office telephone directories and kept the operator slaving. A carefully phrased letter was penned. And, just for good measure on a different matter altogether, she wrote another.

Now she had received a response to the former. A spidery written reply – from Flawbridge! Heck, as the crow flew, that was sort of pretty much down the road.

She threw back her head and shrieked into the blowing wind. "Bindy Bunt, I looking forward to meeting you!" Kicking her heels, she urged Bondi into a gallop. The mare condescended to canter.

Thin faced with a large conk, receding combed back hair, and a dimpled reassuring smile Sir Alec Issigonis observed Gilly through hooded Greek eyes.

She paid scant attention. The photograph of the man that designed the Morris Minor and Jerzy's only non-cricketing hero apart from his dad, hung in the garage workshop's scruffy side office where Gilly floundered with receipts and bank statements. The discrepancies found were alarming.

"Jerzy! Come here. This is awful."

Her son stopped treating Molly's woodworm with a heavy heart. "I thought it was just me. I couldn't make head or tail of it." Nervously he rubbed his rabbit's foot between his oily thumb and forefinger.

"That's not going to do any good. I may be arthritic, but I'm not totally doolally," said Gilly. "We're several hundred pounds light. If you ask me, that wife of yours had her fingers in the till. Losing our money on the paddock was bad enough, but this was under your nose. Didn't you ever think to lock it?"

"This is Snickworthy," he blustered.

"And times they are changin'. Try listening to your Bob Dylan. This isn't what your dad fought for." She covered her eyes with her hands, sniffing to suppress a sob.

Jerzy squeezed her shoulder in an offer of comfort. "Mum, I'm really sorry."

"And it doesn't help you spending your working day repairing vans for free that you've booted the living daylights out of."

"Mum! Margie had just ..."

"Stop yourself right there! I don't want to hear that little thief's name mentioned again. From the very start I guessed she was never pregnant. Women know these things."

"You never said. You never said anything."

Gilly's gander was up. "Would you have listened if I had?" she snapped.

Jerzy flung the rabbit's foot into the floor and stormed out. "I just wanted to do the right thing!" he shouted over his shoulder.

"And don't dare kick Molly!" she called after him, succumbing to more sobs as the garage door clanged.

She drew some quick breaths, pulling herself together, and began shuffling through a pile of receipts she had yet to inspect. Each she ticked off individually against a statement. Nearing the bottom of the pile she gasped. "One 18 carat gold bangle. Paid by cash". The price made Gilly scream.

She and Jerzy would have a poor Christmas.

TWENTY

Saving Bacon

Daffodils trumpeting a new decade of Somerset cricket decorated the stream bank, whilst primroses and celandines were like beacon lights signalling even the most rudimentary sighted mole to erupt with vigour. Barri, no shrinking violet in his sweat sodden T-shirt, was browbeaten by Sir Robert into trundling the heavy roller. Waspishly, he had put George into a sulk.

"They say you can tell it's spring in Zum when a virgin can cover seven daisies with a foot," George had said, idling on the boundary that remained bereft of nets.

In Joy's earshot Barri had replied without putting his brain in gear. "Let's see you do it, then." Battle with the Pitchforkers commenced in a fortnight. Before that the Belters would have played Hogford away. Togetherness was needed.

The pints that later gushed and glugged were, to a point, happily restorative. The Belters, adapting from nursing chilblains to twiddling their fingers on imagined cricket balls, had collected to bibble, or in the cases of Big Doug and Barri to guddle, and to discuss the terms of engagement.

To avoid rumpus Keen Kev had been detained in Rupert's living room to estimate the repair of a problematic sash window. Rupert had prepared a long enough list of questions to occupy a couple of hours.

"It's embarrassing, Kev fawns over her even though she rides like a sack of spuds." said George over his pint, plagiarising his pater's analogy. He tacked on a twist of his own. "Maybe in Kev's heart she's Désirée."

Griffin cringed. "Ooh, that's in bad taste."

George turned to his weekend guest. "Is it in bad taste, Henry? I mean, we're talking potatoes here."

Content in the fug, Henry sat on the fence. "Are we talking about Margie? I didn't think she was a bad sort, meeting her at Lord's. A bit pushy, maybe. But nice enough. Anyway, I wouldn't be in this delightful place now if she hadn't been so sociable" He gave a cordial smile.

"She's a poison dwarf," said Jerzy. He was slowly burying his hatchets on his first outing away from the garage in weeks. Although understandable tensions remained between him and Rupert, Buttercup had emerged from the panel beating and paint job looking in her owner's words "pretty and unabashed".

Big Doug gave a small cough. "Bridey says she's bagged herself a new fancy man." He looked over his shoulder where the new barmaid measured Delvin a double whiskey. "Am I right, Bridey?"

"Wot?"

"Margie, she's got a 'mystery man', you said."

"Hang on." Concentrating, Bridey finished counting the mound of loose change Delvin had rattled onto the bar. "No, I didn't. Said I saw her over by her paddock with a bloke with a tash and briefcase." Jerzy said something undecipherable. "They were chatting about summat," she added.

"A herd," said Griffin to Barri, both absorbed in their own private chat.

Half listening, his mind on the paddock, Jerzy was alarmed. "Pardon?"

"A herd," Griffin repeated. "A group of curlews is called a herd. All that melancholic 'curloo-ooing'. They really milk it … the pity. Cheer up, Mel." He laughed. Very quiet, Mel was not her usual self.

With Jerzy sagging with relief, George took Mel's mention as a cue. "Right, shall we get started? We'll fill Old Willy in when he arrives. So Griffin, as our resident collector of useful facts and as the person who first made contact with our foes, please give us the low-down on the Pitchforkers."

"That's below the belt. First contact came from that effing bull." Griffin's remark was met by a few titters. Big Doug, his conscience niggling, busied himself with a pack of peanuts. Under the table Mel gave him a kick to the shins.

"Where do I start?" mused Griffin. "Um, the Pitchforkers' home turf is a field where Judge Jeffreys orchestrated executions during the Bloody Assizes. Charming. Perhaps, both they and the Belters, given George here's family history, might persuade an umpire to don a black cap prior to raising a digit." Griffin smiled at own jest looking at George for approval and from the scowl he got in return realised he was treading on thin ice.

"Tell us something useful," said George, suddenly prickly.

Griffin made an exaggerated sigh. "I've rung around a few contacts and there's not an awful lot else to tell other than the Pitchforkers are really good. They bowled Hoffy out for eighteen last season."

"Cripes, Hoffy are in Division One," said Big Doug.

"Might have been a dodgy wicket," offered Jerzy.

Griffin quickly dispelled the possible excuse. "Pitchforkers hit two hundred plus."

Mel whimpered.

The door rattled and in burst Old Willy, steward's cap askew, a bundle of wheezing excitement. "Garn, thars a relief. Thought yer all be praper puggle 'eaded by now."

"Pissed? Them? They haven't the cash for drowning sorrows," Bridey ventured.

"Grand news an' thars dazzy-snowt betwaddlin'." Indeed, there was no confusion at all. The preseason ground staff get-together at the County Ground had revealed the concrete. Beefy Botham was captain of England. And the scruffbags had made a celebrated new signing. In as cover for the star West Indians, off on international duty to distant shores, was India skipper Sunny Gavaskar. Knee-high to a grasshopper, the notable batsman had been delighting Test match areas throughout England at the top of India's order. In a short while he could be supping scrumpy but that debate would have to wait.

Big Doug leaned forward. "Match terms were sent to your dad, weren't they, George? Let's hear 'em."

Resolute, George sucked in air through his teeth while rubbing his chin. "Forty overs each side, weather permitting. Minimum overs five. Less than that and it's a six-ball bowl-out – one ball per bowler. Each team to appoint an umpire. Before the toss both animals are to be in pens beside the pitch. Either animal not present will mean it being forfeit to the opposition."

"What happens if either animal ... hypothetically ... goes missing?" said Mel.

"That's also covered." Taking a scrunched piece of paper from his jeans George read aloud. "'Should pedigree pig, known as Wellard, or pedigree highland steer, known as Hairy Fred, be either dead or go missing before the toss then the captain of the team representing the said animal shall be liable to pay a penalty of five hundred pounds to a charity of the opposing team captain's choosing.' I think this covers the point."

Mel was thoroughly peeved. "This has got stupid. It's my pig! I didn't agree to any of that penalty rubbish."

George scratched the back of his head. "Hmm. 'Fraid I *have* agreed. Belters' honour, and all that." He refrained from saying Sir Robert had given him a harsh ultimatum – win the match and restore family pride or vacate Nettlegot until further notice. Kidnapping was an embarrassing blot on family character. Frittering away money to charity was another issue altogether. "Anyway," said George, "Wellard's in rude health and he's good and secure last I looked."

"Then can't we try four-mad-ewe-hairs?" Mel suggested, desperately clutching at straws.

"Force majeure," corrected Griffin, as ever on the ball.

"Yeah, that," said Mel. "How's about unforeseeable actions of badgers digging gurt holes in the pitch?"

In Griffin's opinion hers was an idea to run with. However, he suggested it would be much better to go the whole hog. He cited the example of Headingly in 1975 when campaigners calling for a robber's release stopped the England versus Australia Test match. Not only were holes dug, oil was also liberally poured over one end of the wicket. Jerzy had a lot of oil slopping around his garage, Griffin had said with a wink.

"If memory serves me right," said Henry, "that match was declared a draw. England were robbed of winning back the little Ashes urn. What happens if our game is drawn?"

The answer was on George's thorough bit of paper. "The away team wins."

"Suppose that's fair," said Mel.

"Crazy, the lot of you," said Delvin, now rooting in the depths of his pockets trusting to find sensible coin for another double amongst the piffling halfpennies. He muttered under his breath about loaves and fishes.

"And what about our team? The game will put enormous pressure on Timmy. And Keen Kev's a general liability." Barri seemed to speak for the silent majority.

"Here, here," said Mel. "We can't have him playing for starters." Heads nodded in agreement.

"He won't be," said George, matter-of-factly. "Henry's agreed to play. There's just a chance he might save our bacon." The only sound in the Burning Stump at that split moment was Bridey clinking dirty glasses.

"Well, if that's the case Henry needs to be initiated," announced Rupert grandly. "And to be so in true Belters tradition he must quaff a yard glass of our Jerzy's apple juice. Isn't that right, Jerzy?"

"Totally right, Rupes."

"Er," said George, hesitantly.

"It's okay, George. I don't mind," assured Henry. "I want to feel part of the team and all that."

"You won't feel anything," confided Griffin.

"Griffin, please. Right. Good, good, good. Henry, don't go away. I shall return in two ticks." Rupert was as good as his word.

"This apple juice is made how?" queried Henry, holding the cloudy contents of the yard glass up to the light.

"It's the science of windfalls," said Jerzy. "Sweet or tart, it's as they come. Squeamish folk chop out the worms. I can't be arsed. Once the apples are squidged all that's needed is a hosepipe, muslin, demijohns, bread yeast and bungs. And cotton wool, of course, to stop flies drowning."

"Oh, cotton wool, of course," said Henry. "Cheers."

An hour later, the yard glass long drained and the Belters 'locked-in', Henry was still on the floor doing an admirable impression of an upturned, limb-waggling cockroach. "My legsh," he giggled. "I can't feel my legsh. Shomer-shet-la-la-la."

"You were right, Griff," observed Barri, "Our Henry doesn't even feel a sense a dignity."

"I suggest we all adjourn to the rectory for a few rounds of Black Maria," said Delvin. "I can offer a fine bottle of Irish to anybody else in need of fortification. Volunteers, please, to drag along our guest. Oh, and one other bit of news. Gerald and Jean at the Olde Bakery are leaving us. Gerald said they both wanted to live somewhere 'more connected to the real world'."

A colony of gulls clamoured, laughing – egging on the crows that mobbed a mewing buzzard.

Below, at the summit of the 'top pasture', Henry was on a "tour of the estate". Hung-over and slightly the worse for wear, he loosened his scarlet cravat, and, hands on knees, gasped a lungful of fresh air. "That was so much tougher than the Jubilee Line."

"Told you it'd be worth it, though," said George. "You can see the whole combe from here. What a view, eh?"

"Magnificent. Can I please die?"

"You'll have an audience, if you do. Pater's watching us. Got his binoculars trained. See? Snickworthy's very own border guard. Wave."

As Henry was about to do so Nettlegot became obscured by a mooching line of sheep. A thought struck him. "Don't you have sheepdog? Surely, it's mandatory?" he commented.

"Nope, we've got Lobb the Duckdog, instead – the collie you spoilt at breakfast. Remember?"

"Odd name," said Henry.

"You think so? Did you see how gangly the legs were? The name's just Pater poking fun at the eccentric creature. Back in the Fifties Lobb was a spindle-shanked Zum quickie and, maybe, the greatest number eleven of all time. Certainly Pater thought him the most entertaining. Once tottered back to the pavilion after having his trousers pulled down to 'flagpole' by teammates. Pater saw Lobb run out by deep mid-on – overtook him apparently as he unwisely strolled to the other end. Even Keen Kev hasn't descended yet to such depths of farce. The Duckdog bit's obvious."

"He's for wildfowling, right? Lobb, I mean."

"I wish. And he's actually a she. It's incredible, but she only works India runner ducks – the ones we use to eat the slugs in our veg garden." George looked to the heavens. "Because of Pater's idiocy sheep are off Lobb's roster. Now she does twenty minutes work once a year at the church fête. Folk cheer. Lobb loves it. She's mentally rewired."

Henry's expression showed he was sceptical.

"Honest to goodness, it's true! We had duck poo spread across the outfield where Pater taught Lobb to herd the ducks around bales of straw before penning 'em in a corral of stumps. No Belter would dive to stop a ball for a month. Now Pater dresses up in a smock and straw hat and Lobb's the fête's crowd-pleasing highlight. She's downright smug and wants nothing to do with the ewes anymore – averse to them I suppose. Below her station."

"So, can you cope without a proper sheepdog?"

"Comme ci, comme ça. I improvise with Barri," laughed George. "He isn't half as sniffy. Hey, talk of the devil. I wonder what the secret is. Look, under the copper beech tree – by the pitch roller – Barri's saying something in Joy's ear. Gosh, she's slapped him. Oops." He changed the subject. "Let me help get your bearings, Henry, old chap. Follow my finger – church, Bramble Cottage, Nettlegot, vicarage, Mel's forge, pub, Criddle's garage, the paddock Pater sold that's now you know who's, the Olde Bakery, the Mudworth bungalow, village hall, police house, Loop ... Margie's off somewhere. That's her car – the beige estate heading for the Back Passage. She doesn't normally go anywhere on a Sunday. How interesting."

Even more interesting was Joy holding her tummy and wiping her eyes. Hell.

"What's beyond the wood?" asked Henry.

"Wildlife mostly, red deer and whatnot. If you fancy a set of antlers the stags are shedding them around now. We can go and have a rootle one day. Anyway, let's head downwards to the stone barn and see the lambs."

Almost having let his legs run away with him Henry soon perspired on a pad of cracking concrete nature was set to reclaim much to the delight of some butterflies. "Hey! Tortoiseshells!"

"Mention tortoiseshells again, and I'll hit you," said George.

Henry looked in at the barn's pens wanting the theoretical knowledge gleaned from his bible confirmed. "So a wether lamb means it's castrated?"

"Yep. Snip-snip," said George. "And these are just about ready for the mint sauce".

Henry patted the wall of the stone barn. "Know what? This could make an excellent house. Fab location." It was an off-the-cuff remark. George, however, immediately looked as if he'd seen the manifestation of something holy.

The change coming over his new friend was seen by Henry. "What is it?"

"Nothing. Well, perhaps, it's a thought. I've been racking my brains what would become of me if the Belters lost the match." He explained the situation with Sir Robert.

"And you now intend to live here like a biblical shepherd amongst these woolly boys?"

"Course not. I could convert this place. Be brilliant."

"You told me your dad's stony broke and up the creek without a paddle."

Henry walked to inspect a couple of dilapidations, one of rotting lapped planking, the other of orange and cream-sprayed metal coated in a film of green organic growth. Both had obviously been dumped. The wood sat on its own set of cast iron wheels, its neighbour rested on four breeze blocks. "And I suppose you'd also fill this knackered hen house with prize Cuckoo Marans."

"Why not? They laid James Bond's favourite breakfast egg. 007 liked his Maran's egg boiled for three and a third minutes." Blatantly, Henry was sceptical. "I'm not mucking about, honestly," said George. "It's in the novels. But I reckon they'll need four minutes twenty." He beamed disarmingly.

Henry picked moss from a windscreen wiper. "And you'd probably want to tour the county in this wreck of a camper. Yes?"

"Sarky. Years ago Pater had a go rearing pheasants in that hen house. One night they all vanished. Larry Biggot, our local bobby, wasn't interested. He admitted that up-close pheasants are like autumn leaves, every one different, but he didn't see the point of a magnifying glass. He said Pater should have splodged them with paint – blue, purple, or whatever. Phooph, as if they were moorland sheep. Then the Dapling shoot started when our birds would have been gun ready. Pater firmly believes they added to Biggot's net income. Shabby business. But sort of gives Barri's poaching validation."

"Poaching? Wow. This is like something out of Lady Chatterley." Henry's eyes shone.

"Anyway, the VW camper's Jerzy's," said George quickly. "We had a vision a while back of turning it into the Belters away day bus. Dreams, eh?"

"Umm, absolutely," said Henry before gesturing vaguely toward the rutted track leading off from the barn area. "Where does this lead?"

"It comes out in Church Lane. Not too far from the cricket pitch. You're being very nosy."

"Sorry, George. I don't mean to be ... Hey, isn't that Margie staring at us?"

"Where?"

"Too late. They've gone. Disappeared into the wood."

"They?"

"Looked like she was with a chap. Could have been anyone ... perhaps, Big Doug?" He chortled. "Got a nanosecond glimpse, that's all."

"Must have taken the 'Bluebell Path'. But we saw Margie driving off somewhere. You're sure it was her?"

"Sort of sure – unless fairy Tinkerbell's grown podgy."

"Margie's not that podgy. Maybe it was Jerzy in the car. Then again, given the circumstances, surely not."

"Does it really matter? That it might have been Margie, I mean?"

"Too right! My guess is she's already had the same idea as us. No way is she daft. Once these wethers have gone to market the barn's redundant until autumn. I'm not even sure ... Blast, I have to know who she was with. If the paddock's anything to go by Pater can't go selling land off willy-nilly."

Thoughtful, Henry smoothed his cravat. "Really what you're saying is it's better if it's bought by the right person. Can I have a look inside the hen house?"

"Help yourself. The bolt's a bit stiff."

"Actually the bolt's broken. Screws have been ripped " Prising the door open, Henry stuck in his head. "Ergh! Smells of widdle."

"Sure it's not 'mare's fart'? There's loads of it around." George asked helpfully, taking a whiff of the yellow flowering weeds that encircled the hen house.

"What d'ya mean."

"Mare's fart? I suppose, as a rule, people call it ragwort. I've always known it as mare's fart."

"No, George, it's definitely not mare's fart. You say you only kept chickens and pheasants in here?"

"Yep."

"Did any of them wee in milk bottles or suck humbugs? And you've got mighty big woodworms." Henry re-emerged, gave a shiver, and went to closely investigate the endemic ragwort.

"You're a glutton for punishment," commented George.

"Come here," Henry invited. "Look there. What do you see?"

George peered. "Nothing, just a bit of saw dust."

"Exactly. See these two holes? They were clearly made by someone inside wanting a good view of the barn. Can't believe your wethers are that interesting. So I reckon you've got yourself a peeping Tom. What *do* you get up to here?"

"Nothing. Honest." said George indignantly, doing an admirable impression of a Somerset beetroot.

"Well, somebody's been making an exhibition of themselves."

A slender weasel poked a twitching nose and beady eyes out of a rusty hole in the caravanette's door, saw company, and darted back chattering. A forewarning wind swayed a patch of red campion. Behind the men's backs dark storm clouds crept.

TWENTY-ONE

Fatal Revelation

Not that Margie had let on, but the planning officer's visit had been a travesty of brutal honesty. Getting rich quickly was pie in the sky and, having wintered poorly, meant coming to terms. Approval for the paddock to become a plot for bungalows was doubtful. Written villager protests would snuff it. In her head she already heard the scratching of nibs.

However, the salacious snap of her mother and Larry Biggot coerced Bondi's feed as well as her own rent, and she could still draw the bowstring of discord to twang targeted revenge at the Belters bigwigs.

Now a bit of fortune would do wonders.

From the outside the terraced house looked bleak and cramped – a bad sign. "Knock-knock," she called, putting her head around the front door that opened in off the street, disturbing tumbleweeds of fluff. "It's Margie Bobowski, Mrs Bunt. I've come as promised."

"Come in, dear. No need to shout. I'm just here," said a reedy voice from a tall backed armchair.

Faded wallpaper, 1950s' butterflies and ballerinas, blistered in places and peeled in others. Net curtains were as grubby as the single window. Nice hovel. "Hi," said Margie shaking the offered liver-spotted, skeletal claw. She blenched at the signs of age – the grey hair, the wizened features, skin temple tight, and unkempt clothes that swamped. "What a crone," she thought, wrinkling her nose. The house had a musty smell of pee and lavender. Linen doilies on the low table, in Margie's opinion, desperately needed a boil. The crumbly cake was clearly stale. Margie felt downhearted. What if Bindy was the last of the line?

"Mrs Bunt. Bindy. May I call you Bindy? Thank you for replying to my letter."

"It was quite a surprise. Nobody's asked if the Bunts are descended from the West Somerset Snooks before. I was inquisitive. Help yourself to a piece of walnut. Homemade, though not by me, I'm afraid."

Margie raised the palm of her hand. "Looks lovely, Bindy. But I must think about my figure."

She didn't want to dive straight in with the big questions so she looked around for an icebreaker. Horse brasses, or something naff like a china carthorse dragging a sherry bottle, perhaps. There was nothing remotely in that vein. Indeed, the dingy lounge offered small inspiration, apart from a crude painting of a kangaroo. Best not to compliment that.

The balls of red and blue wool and a weird socky thing spawned by Bindy's clicking needles would have to do. "That's a funny shape you're knitting?"

"This? It's a winter woolly for my friend's buff Orpington duck. Terrible thing. Had a nasty fright from a mink." She patted a plump cushion and winked. "The feathers are in here ... Your face! I'm only joking. You are a bit gullible, dear."

"The Snook name's long gone, and sadly I'm the last Bunt ..."

It was a dead end.

Margie felt as if she'd been hit by flying partridge. She needed to collect her thoughts. Bindy, though, caught her devastation. "Oh, don't look like that. Cheer up." She poked her knitting. "This is actually going to be a tea cosy for my grandson."

"Honestly?" said Margie, now keenly alert.

"Honestly."

Thank goodness for that, thought Margie. "Did you know your grandson may have rights to some property that once belonged to the Snooks?"

"Since you put it that way, yes, I suppose so."

Margie clenched her fists.

"But the Snooks lived such a long time ago, dear. I still don't see why you're so interested."

"It's just that I love history, local stuff especially," said Margie.

Perhaps because of the gloom she didn't notice the shrewd look in Bindy's eye, nor the rub of fingers well capable of tickling trout.

"Have you an open mind, my dear?"

"Oh, yes, very," said Margie, eagerly.

"I'm sure you do. Though not quite as open as my grandson's, I hope. He's not the brightest cabbage in the patch. None too helpful if you're an orphan." Bridey saw Margie's mind was ticking and continued. "Before the boy could walk, my daughter Edna went to Australia with Ted, my son-in-law. Left my grandson behind promising she would fetch him when he was older. Tragically, Ted fell into a baling machine. Nothing left but four toes. My daughter died from a broken heart."

Margie glanced again at the kangaroo. "Why did they go to Australia?"

"There had been an accident. I'm not sure if I should tell you this – Ted mistook someone wearing a driving coat and leather cap and goggles for a gentleman ... oh, not like you're thinking."

"I'm thinking Lady Rosemary," said Margie.

"Oh my dear, you *are* good."

"Course, I've never told my grandson any of this. Thought it best not to. Draw a veil, I say, me dear.

"Mrs Bunt, I disagree. He totally deserves to know. Everybody has a right to know where they've come from. Mrs Bunt? Please don't fall asleep. Speak to me. Who is your grandson? It'll be our secret."

"What harm can there be, I suppose. I'm so sleepy, me dear. Maybe, it's best if you come back tomorrow."

Margie ground her teeth and simpered. "Mrs Bunt, just say and I'll leave you to rest. It's been so kind of you to see me. Who is your grandson?"

"You must know. He lives so local to you. It's ..." Bindy gave a huge yawn.

"Would you like some walnut cake? I can't remember if I asked you."

"NO! … No thank you, Mrs Bunt." The old lady yawned, again. Margie feared her falling into the sleep of the dead. "Maybe the tiniest piece. It looks *so* good." Margie popped a crumb into her mouth and hoped saliva would soften it. "Mrs Bunt, what's your grandson's name?"

"It's Kevin of course. Kevin Furet. Your landlord? Sadly, he lacks gumption and is easily led." Margie completely missed the wrinkled poker-face. Ted aside, Bindy's grandad, too, had tried culling a virile Wimble-Clatt. By ridiculous coincidence the bungler had instead seen off the wife. What was her name? She had to think. Ah yes, Lady Maud. "A piece of advice, Mrs Bobowki. If you want something never give up."

Margie had no intention to. Her vision had clarity. And for first things first, Big Doug was a godsend. In Bindy's grotty parlour she almost did a rain-dance.

TWENTY-TWO

Weather Warning

Thunder rumbled like a drum roll in the heavens. Blown in from the Bristol Channel, the rain, which had been coming and going, now spattered in big gobs upon creatures of paw, trotter, hoof, and claw. Near the village glimmer a lightning flash illuminated a grubbing badger. Snuffling as if from a heavy cold it bullied a hedgehog away from a bonanza of churchyard earthworms.

Perched in the great copper beech a barn owl flexed its talons spying supper in the glossy darkness. Below, where the outer branches overhung the boundary edge, a vole scurried passed Barri's roller and between emerging molehills.

The swoop silent and unerring cut short the squeak of panic. The vole's demise was almost imperceptible as the squall intensified, plothering down to coat Sir Robert's bedroom window with sheen as thick and opaque as glycerine.

Under his blankets he tossed and turned unable to sleep. His gout was uncomfortable and he was berating himself as he had done for years and years, reliving the scene – Rosemary coyly nibbling her pork crackling, fluttering her lashes and pouting she "died to see the new Dennis Price" and couldn't wait a day longer. That was just minutes before his planned departure for the otter hunt. Like the lovesick fool he was, he had caved in even after having crowed at the Harvest Festival about "braving the Wednesday afternoon's Exmoor weasel patrols for the sheer gall of chasing Tarka".

There were other reasons for him to chastise himself. The boundary net fund had proved too big a temptation when the electric bill became excessively overdue. However, this was a just a minor niggle compared to how he had treated George. He dearly loved his son but had never told him so. He was proud of the way George worked his arse off in the losing battle to keep the body and soul of Nettlegot together. And he had not told George that either.

Now the situation was dire and he had been cruel to be kind. Chances of the Belters winning the stupid match, he believed, were nil. The Pitchforkers would be chomping on cigars within ten overs. However, using the game as an excuse was lame. Perhaps he should have been blunt. Nettlegot Ned, the prize ram – in truth, second in the local show – didn't cut the mustard for more than a pony. So either a chunk of the estate got sold soon or they were virtually broke.

Because of pride, self-respect, embarrassment or pure funk – call it what you will – he hadn't been honest. The only person he had confided in over Nettlegot's misfortune was Aunt Frances. Worst coming to worst, she offered George a bolt-hole and a catering job – wellies and wethers to be substituted for a dicky bow and trays of canapés and champers.

That offer was in the letter of "the kidnap" highlight, an event Aunt Frances pressed to have found "totally hilarious". Misleading George was heartless. And he'd gilded the lily over the Queen of Denmark. That was a step too far. Had his wife been alive, he dared not think of the bollocking he'd have got for being so underhanded.

On his bedside table Lady Rosemary posed on the wing of the sports car. Unseen in the dark a droplet trickled down the glass of the photo frame, chased by another.

Fatigue led Sir Robert into fitful slumber. He lounged in the leather armchair. Slimed and bloodied George birthed a lamb on the hearth mat. Lissom, accoutred in a sexy corset and frilly pantaloons, Joy gave him succour.

His gaze went from her cleavage to the window. "There's a pig on the cricket pitch, large as life!" he exclaimed, failing to draw his son's attention to it. The lamb had transformed into a badger cub and George was swinging it pendulum fashion by the hindquarters. Flustering with a polka dot cravat, Joy tried to wipe mucus from the cub's mouth.

"Look at the pig! Get it off before it damages the wicket." He felt panicked.

"The wretched thing's having a crap at the stream end. Move, George."

"Why bother," said Joy, her face suddenly up close. "They start building the bungalows tomorrow. You've sold our cricket field, you silly fool." He stared about the room. Ancestors were grim in their gilded frames. Among them Great Grandad Arthur in his cricket garb scowled furiously. Tucking the cub under one arm George offered canapés. "Prawn and mayonnaise, and devilled kidney. Help yourself Pater." He reached for a devilled kidney, managing to drop it on his lap. "Here, have this, too." George let go of the cub.

"Argh, take it away. It's piddling on me!"

Sir Robert woke up confused, heart racing. There was a weight on his upper legs. The blanket was wet. He fumbled for the light switch on the wall behind the bed. Flick. Pop! In the blue flash instant he saw a gape in the ceiling. Flick-flick. Flick-flick. Darkness.

Along the landing in the pitch black Henry's head fell back onto the pillow. An ammonite fossil he had found in the chest of drawers gave comfort. He fondled it in a hand as the storm continued to batter his window. Adding further brilliant notions into his Molskine would have to wait till morning. Before then, excited, mind ticking, he doubted any possibility of falling asleep. But sleep he did, dreaming of sea monsters and secret agents, cricket tea, chocolate, egg sandwiches and strumming his guitar to an audience of lambs.

❖ ❖ ❖

The chalice drained, the purificator was folded moist with wine dribbles. The audience with the bishop niggled. The only thing likely to rattle the collection plate was a rebounding delivery.

Preparing for the season ahead Delvin practiced off breaks down the nave. "Drat. One more go." He skipped after his worn, yellow tennis ball that had rolled under the table stacked high with damp hymn books. He massaged his wrist, adjusted his cassock and stroked his beard. Beginning below the pulpit, from a short angled run up to miss the puddle, he gave the ball an extra tweak. Finally, it avoided the edge of the uneven flagstone, missed the pew end, sharp turned passed the granite Labrador paw cornering the Wimble-Clatt tomb, and hit the font pedestal plumb. The ball had travelled exactly twenty-two yards.

The small impact created an odd echo. "Howzat!" said Delvin. No echo. Very odd.

"Alright, vicar?" Entering unnoticed Keen Kev, rain-soaked and sweaty, flicked his squirrel tail menacingly. "Better give the floor a mop before communion. But, little point me doing it with mud on my shoes. Best I use the scraper outside," he said disappearing behind the curtain that separated the entrance between nave and tower.

"Whatever you say, Kev."

Delvin heard Keen Kev opening the tower door before hearing a thud and a howl. "Kev?" Not a sound. "Kev? You okay?" Delvin dashed to discover Keen Kev lying prostrate on the tower step, his flat cap in a puddle. Rain matted the sidesman's hair and ran in rivulets from the bridge of his nose, around his eyes and mouth, to trickle down his neck and seep under his collar. Nuzzled against him grinned the grotesque stone head of the fang lacking hunky punk. From underneath poked the squirrel tail.

Had he been too blasé since Big Doug's bludgeon? Cripes, the creature had leered over Snickworthy through four hundred years of storm and tempest. Delvin had a cold sweat coming on.

Clasping a wrist he felt for a pulse. "Hallelujah." He checked for blood and saw none. The cheeks were rosy, another good sign. Same old weasel. Grabbing under the armpits he dragged the soggy limpness across the threshold into the church and stuck a prayer hassock under Keen Kev's noggin. Delvin cursed first Big Doug, secondly the weather, then both together.

Keen Kev groaned.

"Kev? Thank goodness. Can you hear me? You're fine. I think you fainted from shock."

"I want compensation. Lots," mewled Keen Kev, eyes still closed. His chest rose and fell a few times. Then, having held silence for a long moment, added: "Did you know I'm a Snook?"

"You're delusional."

"No I'm not, vicar. Nettlegot's mine. By rights."

"You're blathering like a loon."

"I saw you, vicar. You and your fancy woman."

There was a sudden flapping in the doorway as Joy shook rainwater off her practical umbrella and a bunch of daffodils. "What an ugly visitation on the doorstep. Morning, both."

Delvin was taken aback. "Joy, can't you see Kev's had a nasty fright? The blessed hunky punk could have been his ticket to the Gates of Saint Peter."

"Oh toosh," said Joy. "That was quite a pantomime, Kev."

Keen Kev moaned dramatically.

"Stop putting it on, Mr Furet. Worrying the vicar to death is quite unfair."

The invalid became a tad petulant. "I'm not putting anything on."

"I advise that you do, Mr Furet. Something dry. If you stay in those wet clothes you may well suffer a bout of 'pew-moanier' – an Old Willyism." She smiled pitilessly. "I saw your antics from the lychgate."

"And I saw you, Miss Budd."

Was it just him or did Keen Kev's voice carry a smidgen of threat? "Joy? What's going on?" asked Delvin, confused.

"You'll be surprised," said Joy whose sudden blush had become puce. "Please just check the steps up to the belfry. And if you're feeling brave clamber the ladder and search the tower top."

Delvin regarded her curiously.

"Please, D ... Delvin" she insisted.

"Right you are." Donning his beret, and without further question, Delvin did as asked.

Propping himself on an elbow Keen Kev moved to get up. Joy wagged a finger. "You worm. Stay right where you are while I find a vase for my poor daffs."

Heavy treads descending the stairwell announced Delvin's return. "I found mysterious wet footprints," he wheezed. "And this heavy beast." He parked a sledgehammer on a flagstone. "Discovered it lying beside the parapet that faces the cricket pitch. I think I'm beginning to comprehend what's happened."

"Then I shall make it blatantly clear," said Joy. "Mr Furet climbed the tower, and tonked the head off the hunky punk. Obviously he came down because I saw him lift the head from the churchyard mud and fake his elaborate little accident. A howl worthy of am-dram, I thought. And a nice detail, Mr Furet, dropping the head on your squirrel tail. I know how you treasure that revolting thing. So that wasn't your idea, was it? So let me guess. Margie Bobowski?"

Grim faced, Delvin looked at the abject person now rocking backwards and forwards on his bum, knees clutched to chest. "Have you got anything to say for yourself?"

Keen Kev blinked owlishly. "I'm a Snook."

"Whilst *you* decide what you are I must get ready for communion," responded Delvin matter-of-factly. "Joy, can you ring the Daplings and ask that they send Timmy to tug a vacant bell rope for the eleven o'clock?" He glowered at Keen Kev who looked up with puppy dog eyes. "I almost feel inclined to attach your neck. Can't believe it's still only seven-thirty." That by itself made things even odder in Delvin's mind. Yes, it was early, but it certainly wasn't dark and that made no sense.

Keen Kev had gone potty as a herb – strange. Stranger still he had done so in murky daylight, around the time of Joy's habit of doing the church flowers. Delvin doubted the 'luck' in witnessing the wanton destruction. And, well in range of Sir Robert's binoculars, it was perfectly feasible to have been seen from Nettlegot. Ludicrous. It was as if Keen Kev had wanted to get caught.

On the face of it, however, Keen Kev and Margie posed a very real threat to village harmony – his fault in truth. Matters should have been nipped in the bud with the fedora. He and Joy needed to be proactive. Not a panacea, but certainly things might well be easier.

A china teacup jiggling in its saucer made Henry open his eyes to the land of the living and his ears to bells. "Hope you've brought your galoshes. That was quite a night," said Joy cheerily. "I've been to church and George's been up and sploshing around the cricket pitch with our Barri for ages. The stream's broken its bank and it's still raining. Nettlegot's become a sieve. Glad to see you don't need a saucepan. Every bucket and pail's commissioned. I had to evacuate Sir Robert to the downstairs sofa. He's got the screaming habdabs. So don't go too close."

"Garlic and wolfsbane," Henry joked, signing a cross. "What time is it?"

"Raise yourself in the next ten minutes and we can still call it breakfast, later than that and it'll have to be brunch. Sorry, but we've no electric. Thank goodness the Aga boils a kettle. The phone's working should you fancy contact with civilization."

"Country life, eh?" said Henry rubbing his eyes and sitting up. Bashfully buttoning his open pyjamas he felt oddly chipper.

"And as of this Sunday morning you're not our only guest," said Joy. "Prebendary Wickham invited himself and he's not budging. If you'd like to meet him he's outside the French windows." She laughed.

Henry took a sip of tea. "Shall we say brunch? I would like to make a couple of calls, if that's okay. Then if you can muzzle Sir Robert I'd love to corner him for a word. Right, action stations." He flung off the bedclothes.

A mallard pair splash landed at cover point.

"Wedi'r cwbl, the moles are snorkelling." Squelching in the middle of the wicket Barri moaned from under his anorak hood. "Fancy aquatic sports,

George? Water polo? Yachting? I sure there'll be trout at long leg. At least let me put that cock fezzie out its misery."

"Nope. Wickham's off limits."

"Strewth, naming a bird's stupid."

"No it's not. Anyway, Wickham suits him. He looks long-suffering and his white collar's ruddy admirable."

"George, listen, it's just a bird."

"No, you listen for once. Bet you didn't know the honorary canon was Zum's gauntleted stumper when Grace knocked his hundredth hundred. Bristol 1895. The Big 'Un celebrated his achievement with champers. It so pepped him up that he went on to hit two-hundred-and-eighty-eight in three-hundred-and-twenty minutes. Only four balls passed the good doctor's bat during his entire innings. Rest of the time the only thing in Archie Wickham's line of sight was W.G.'s bum. So if this bird came seeking sanctuary, sanctuary is what he'll receive."

"You're going barmy. Nettlegot's not sanctuary to man or bird, it's falling to pieces. And aren't you forgetting the fezzie season's over? The guns are silent till October."

"When has that ever stopped you?"

"It's just a bloody pheasant!"

"To you, maybe. And that's my worry."

"But there're zillions of the sodding pea-brainers."

George was grateful for a distraction doing justice to a Cheshire cat appearing outside the French windows. "Ah, I see Henry's up at last, and Wickham isn't bothered by him." Indeed, man and bird seemed joined as rapt observers. "C'mon, give him a wave."

Keeping cold mitts in damp pockets Barri blew out his cheeks. "What with? All this water? Can't see me getting this pitch ready in time for the Pitchforkers. And I can do without the spectators." He clapped his hands. Startled, the ducks took flight quacking their pique. Wickham, however, was unmoved. "Maybe it's just deaf. Sure complement a blind bull."

"Know what? Maybe pheasants have the genetic homing instinct of salmon."

"Bollocks. I'm off for a brew." Before Barri could enjoy that, however, he would have to empty out the acorns submerged in his rainwater filled tea mug.

Bedraggled, George knew he smelled like a wet dog. Henry's announcement, though, he found harder to rationalise. "Obviously the barn'll need planning permission. With five acres, the henhouse and four ewes for starters it'll be perfect. I'll want to name the sheep after Zum players. You can help me, there."

The minor details were flying over George's head and he felt dizzy, needing the support of the billiard table. "And Pater's actually agreed to sell?"

"Verbally and once the wethers have gone to market, yes. Snatched my hand off at the ballpark figure. Your dad's suggested I stay at Nettlegot until after the Pitchforkers game to start the actual ball rolling. As a thank you, and as we're probably all a bit rusty, I'm donating the Belters a cricket net. We'll have you walloping Delvin's googlies before he starts sermonising next week."

"How kind." George, however, wasn't to be distracted by such niceties. "That barn's built for the four-legged, not to be lived in by a human."

"So an architect needs finding. Gotta have conversion plans drawn up to discuss with the planning bods. Of course, things need tying together with my London flat. I accepted the offer I've been prevaricating upon…" Henry checked his watch "… fifteen minutes ago."

"Lummy," said George, peering numbly at a large stain in the corner of the ceiling. "And any plans for having a dry roof over your head for the foreseeable future?"

"Absolutely. I'm going to hire a caravan. Stockbroker to gypsy, and the proud owner of Folly Farmyard. Isn't it a grand address?"

George suddenly felt in a bit of a huff. His inheritance was in danger of shrinking from a double duvet to a dishcloth and at the true root of it, he realised, was Margie. "Where's Pater now?"

"In his chair, I think, making a wine list. Shall I open a window a little? It's quite stuffy."

"As is Wickham if he gets in," said George, grateful for Henry's tact.

"Anyone feeling peckish?" asked Joy, entering the billiard room with a tray of cheese and cold meat sandwiches.

"Always," said George. "Heard the news? Henry is buying the stone barn. He plans to live in it."

The crash of the tray scared Wickham to clattering flight.

"Idiot!" To her mind Keen Kev's task hadn't been difficult and her idea brilliant. She gave Bondi a crack of the crop. The mare protested. Margie cracked harder. Then, as the obvious dawned, she yanked severely on the bit.

It was she who was the idiot not Keen Kev. Course there was no proof either way. None. Just his word against Delvin's and Joy's. But woe betide the Belters. A fool could see the hunky punk head had simply fallen off. Could have killed. That was her story and Daddy would delight in seeing it headlined.

Keen Kev, too, had better stick to it for his own benefit. She would ram it home in the safety of Bramble Cottage. Then something magnificent flashed across her thoughts. Had he other smutty snapshots squirrelled away? Very likely. And dosh, hopefully, too.

A house search wouldn't go amiss before the local deadline.

TWENTY-THREE

Pool of Exposure

Riding roughshod over his wishes she had visited his gran. Now she had broken her word. Envious of his garden snails whose homes were their own he hadn't the backbone to ask Margie to leave.

Neither cuddles nor percentage looked to be forthcoming. No surprise there. From the bedroom window the decapitated hunky punk stood out like a sore thumb. Bramble Cottage had an atmosphere reeking of horse and nail varnish. And Keen Kev had a cold in his head and utterly cold feet.

"Barri locked me in the hen house. So he definitely knows. Probably gave myself away when Botham got his hundredth Test wicket."

An odd gargling arose in Margie's throat.

Its water boiling, the kettle whistled, rattled its lid and spouted steam, providing Keen Kev an excuse to disengage from his grilling and make his gran's cure-all.

Margie had calculated on him turning out for Henry's first net practice. He promised her he would – even changed into his whites. However, as he did in the church tower, he procrastinated – this time at the stile in Church Lane as a band of Belters lined up to bowl at Mel. George went first and was whacked straight to the stream. Henry ribbed her. Why bother providing a spanking new net if she chose to ignore it?

Keen Kev couldn't see Delvin. Timmy, ignorant, gave him a thumbs up. Then the sight of Barri showing two fingers had made him flunk out, forlorn. Hence he had caught Margie with her hands in the tomato juice cupboard. Betting he had a secret stash of cash somewhere was a bet she had lost. Second best was more than passable. Brazenly she'd laid his Polaroids on the kitchen surface and admired a wealth of bare skin.

Shame overwhelmed him.

The time was passed of him doffing his cap, and he deeply regretted having her in a house that seemed no longer his. The kitchen, once homely, no longer smelled of boiled onions. Her gubbins were strewn about every ledge and into every corner and the floor was a mess. Sight of his squirrel tail – the sole thing he had been given by his father – had her screaming. The radio played pop. Since carelessly biffing the India rubber ball through the hole in the hedge the rug of his existence had been pulled from under him.

So what if he was a Snook? Judas of the Belters was who he really was.

"I never set out to take all these," he mumbled, feeling the urge to pour the contents of the kettle over his handiwork.

"Don't even think it," said Margie icily. And there lay the problem. She was always one step ahead of him. "You found that foul hen house compulsive, I know you did, you dirty man."

Keen Kev felt the sting. "The vicar's a lecher," he blurted. "I saw him at it. I just wanted proof. It's not Christian the way he carries on." But to be honest, since Margie had played with his head, he wouldn't care less if the vicar was Lucifer fallen. "You silly thing, there's no wriggle-room. Bash it and play dead. I'll take care of the rest," she'd persuasively said.

Do as she insisted and she might soon disappear. That had been his hope. What he wouldn't give just to be the butt of batting jokes again, and have his Sunday fun keeping Mrs Dapling awake.

He poured the hot water into a mug and added a glug of cider vinegar, a teaspoon of sugar and a cinnamon stick.

Margie wanted to be absolutely certain of the spanner chucked into her calculations. "So Clewes didn't call Officer Biggot, is that what you're saying?"

"Not that I know of. I'm a criminal, either way." He felt on the brink of tears. "You've twisted me."

"Are we feeling sorry for our self? As I recall I wasn't the one with the sledge-hammer. We help each other, Kev. Remember, you don't want me as an enemy."

The chill he was enduring just got worse. There had to be a way for his side of the story to be heard.

Upstairs in Number 6, The Loop, Ollie painted a starry sky on Lili's ceiling. Downstairs with little to do, Wedgy slept and Lili absorbed herself with her 'fairy pigs' – woodlice on a bed of moss which Ollie had found and put in a matchbox – while Bridey and Polly, having opened a bottle of red, revelled in a girlie chat. Inevitably the subject matter turned to love life.

"Cor, I'm spoiled for choice," said Bridey. "Mummy's boy Jerzy, Rupert and Big Doug, phooaar! Miss Molly, Miss Buttercup and Miss bloody Bumpkin might have summat to say, mind. And I forgot gawky Griffin. But, well, he's got the prissy *Pertelote*."

"Any bloke you *really* fancy," giggled Polly, stubbing ash from her roll-up. "How's about George? He's hunky. Big House. Very eligible."

Bridey wrinkled her nose. "Nah, too whiffy, and bit of a prat. A nice prat, though."

"That's my knight in shining armour you're dissing. How he yanked me over the wall at the cricket ground, a maiden in distress – that was so funny. When Ollie gets randy he's all paws ... You should have seen his face! There was me thinking I was taking him to a nice romantic corner that's like ... I dunno ... a secret garden dripping with ivy, and George goes and says it's a plague pit. Imagine! I can't forget the great time I had ... at the cricket ... the excitement and everything. Seeing Viv Richards and Botham ... it was just brill." Polly chewed at a fingernail.

"Top up?" said Bridey pouring more wine. "There's something between him and the blonde bitch, poison dwarf. Nothing serious. She's proper dodgy.

Ain't she, Wedgy?" The Staffy twitched an ear. Bridey lowered her voice conspiratorially. "Pol, do yer still have crush on him? George?"

"I haven't seen him. Have I?" Polly said.

"That ain't what I asked."

Polly blushed.

"Yer do, yer dark horse!"

"Shush." Polly glanced anxiously at the ceiling.

Wincing with a grin Bridey's volume became sotto voce. "I thought yer did when you were staring over the fence that day. Remember? When the gurt bloke hit the goblinny thing?"

"Actually, I was thinking about how nice the big house would look with a rose garden. I even designed one with shaped beds and trellises. Got inspired by Sanssouci. Took me hours. I imagined George in a periwig like he was Frederick the Great."

"Get on!"

"Straight up."

"Show it to him, then – yer sons-oozy piccy. Come to the match over that woman's pig."

Polly giggled, again. "Can't … no, can't … anyway, I've got Ollie … You haven't said who you fancy."

"Yeah, yeah. Well, there's Barri, the bloke with the scar, he's quite fit."

"Quite? Look at *you*," jested Polly. This time it was Bridey that flushed. Both of them giggled.

"But, but, but," said Bridey. "Henry's gorgeous."

They clinked their wine glasses.

The first to draw attention had been Mrs Dapling. Unable to track down Larry Biggot within five minutes, she had entered the Stump for the only time in her life. And she was perturbed. "Mr Shovelton," she said finding Rupert alone and hassling him from the cricket reports, "Kevin Furet has locked himself in the lock-up and he won't come out until 'someone listens', he says. And I can't get my morning paper."

"Oh good grief. Well, he can't have been there very long. I only picked up mine in the past half hour. Think positively – no news is good news. He'll come out when he needs a pee."

"Please Mr Shovelton, if my hubby doesn't have his crossword I get it in the niddick. There must be a quick solution."

"Humane killer or the vicar?"

"Mr Shovelton! This is important."

"For crying out loud. So is Somerset versus Sussex." He put down his daily with grim reluctance. "Okay, Mrs Dapling, at your persistence I'll go and have a word."

TWENTY-FOUR

Quacklets and Crocks

Elsewhere, the scruffbags' season was already up and running in-between the drenching April showers. And the Demon of Frome had the best scruffbag bowling figures of his life. Good signs, bolstered by reports from Old Willy that the arrival of Sunny Gavaskar was imminent. Tagging along would be a retinue of servants. Apparently, neither Sunny nor wife had the foggiest notion how to cook and wash.

It was a criticism George, on occasions, unkindly had levelled at him by Barri, whose mower roared over the problematic cricket pitch dandelions keeping them under control before he jumped aboard the Bumpkin. Roof down the car was braving it and Hogford bound. His: "Sure you're on the right side today. Mel?" was met with the friendly riposte: "Go twiddle."

"We're a man short. Apologies from Keen Kev" said Griffin for Barri's benefit "He left an odd message with Rupes saying he can't play."

Mel laughed from the front passenger seat, "We knew that!"

Undistracted, Griffin carried on with the announcements. "Henry is having his first outing and has gone in Molly, helping Old Willy and Delvin cuddle a flagon of Jerzy's scrumpy. Buttercup holds the usual gruesome twosome."

Seize the moment, thought Barri, having one final chew of his lip. Here we go - Joy's say so. Barri spoke loudly into the on-rush of springtime air. "About Keen Kev not playing; that's to do with Sir Robert's hen house and your hunky punk, Doug."

"Pardon Barri? Can't hear you there on the back seat. Tell me later. *Blackbird*!"

Hand on illusory wyvern, Big Doug belted out the refrain. "Where be that Blackbird to? I know where he be, he be up yon Wurzel tree, and I be after eeeEEE!"

Her brakes slammed on, the Bumpkin skidded and stalled.

"Ow, my neck's cricked," moaned Mel. "No, ow, it's worse than that."

"My bloomin' eye," Griffin complained, having whopped the back of Big Doug's head. "Doug, you oversized numpty."

"Not my fault." Breathing heavily Big Doug slumped over the steering wheel.

A mother mallard, head probably full of family matters, had chosen the Bumpkin's high-speed approach as the ideal moment to lead her brood of ducklings across the lane in search of paddling puddles. Big Doug laboured out of the driver's seat. Fearing the worst, he peered around the bonnet.

"No harm done. No flat quacklets," he called, relieved. "Come on, you cutie." Bending down he encouraged a fluffy laggard with a flick of his middle finger towards the peeps of its brethren.

Reunion complete he tried returning to the vertical. "Oh, sugar plums." His back had gone.

"Great. Only in Somerset," sighed the unscathed Barri. "If I had a pot of red paint handy I'd daub a cross on the bonnet."

"I heard what you said about our squirrel-tailed one," Griffin muttered to him.

"Good. Delvin wants urgent words with you after the match."

"Reckon he'll have a piece of rare beefsteak about him?" grimaced Griffin gently prodding his rapidly purpling shiner. "And we already know about Keen Kev lurking in the hen house. Henry told us after net practice. I think you'd already buggered off to canoodle with Bridey."

"We didn't canoodle."

"Whatever ... Doug, grin and bear it and get yourself into the back. I think this one-eyed pirate better drive. Barri, are you ever going to bother learning? What did they teach you in the army?"

"Nothing of any use," Barri muttered, suddenly sombre, hearing explosions in his head as Griffin slammed the Bumpkin's driver's door.

Mel commenced with language fruitier than Jerzy's scrumpy. The gist being that within the week Wellard's fate now rested with a bunch of crocks, voyeurs, and incompetents.

Hogford's captain was understanding. The waiting Belters were astonished at the effect of a duck. That the team lost aided by a pair of non-combatant 'borrows' yet to experience teenage surprised no one.

"Please, let him go, Mel," said Rupert, in the wake of the trouncing and the effects of Jerzy's scrumpy. "You'll have him joining the walking wounded." Overcoming her neck pain the huge hug Mel gave Henry for scoring a faultless fifty and taking a 'five-for' risked crushing her hero's ribcage.

"Oi, Griffin," Delvin tugged a shirtsleeve to gain the attention of the back-slapping Belter. "Let's take a short walk."

The catcall from Mel was inappropriate.

The hunky punk saga was going to run. Gunning the *Pertelote's* little outboard Griffin headed for deep water with a queasy, chastened passenger in the bow seat, a pair of fishing rods, and a box of tackle and bait. Asked to do a bit of trawling, he was obliging.

"Bit lumpy. Can't be helped," he called down the boat, making himself heard over the throbbing engine.

Delvin's deduction was surely right, he thought. Despite the elaborate show Keen Kev was nabbed as easily as a whelk. Griffin stuck by his belief the bloke wasn't inherently bad. Being a tad overzealous with a squirrel tail was irritating, but no crime. And, plain as a huss is a dogfish, he had a passion for the summer game. That he was useless at it was nobody's fault, although

Mel was naughty in forever dousing any flickering embers of fortitude.

Equally plain had been Keen Kev's crush on Margie. The result was glaringly obvious. She had played the proprietor of Blackberry Windows with greater aplomb than he could execute the forward defensive, and he had been kippered.

The 'Snickworthy Bicycle' was an apt name for her. Griffin was chuffed to have thought of it. Others, like Jerzy, had been taken for a ride. And, according to Rupert, George almost so. The issue was money. It was always about money. Griffin checked himself. No, that wasn't absolutely true. She had made an exception for Barri - the Snickworthy Lothario.

On the distant foreshore rocks cormorants hung out dripping wings to dry. A shag dived not far from the boat. Fish. Griffin cut the motor. The Snook question was one of several needing an answer. The possibility of George and Keen Kev being related, albeit as distantly as his line between fishhook and reel, gave Griffin the urge to reach for his stinky bait-box. Lesser black-backed gulls and kittiwakes yelped their encouragement.

Griffin offered his guest who was white as one of Joy's laundered sheets a seasickness tablet, a hip flask and a rod. "Well, Kev, here we are, just you and me. Time to get things off your chest."

Aided by a tot of apple brandy Keen Kev swallowed and regarded the rod and its trappings doubtfully. "Never done this before. Fishin'."

"Clears the head. Honestly, you'll find it easier than batting. Watch and learn. Just simple practice." Griffin fed out some reel line, selected a lead weight and a swivel, cut a line of trace, impaled a piece of squid on a hook, and tied things in order with expert knots. "There. All yours. Keep your thumb on the reel and let the line out slowly ... not too fast ... perfect. Fishy, fishy, fishy."

Rolling a ciggy Griffin let Keen Kev be for a while and watched a parcel of oystercatchers in flight. One of their number left dawdling did its best to catch up. "Pink-a-pink-a-pink," it clamoured. "Alright, out with it," Griffin said, at last aware of colour returning to Keen Kev cheeks. "What's been going on? From the top, please."

Keen Kev gushed tumbling words that were suspended by a line tug.

"Well done!" said Griffin. "Reel in slowly. Three turns. Relax. Give slack. Three turns. That's the way. I wonder what you've got."

Before too long Griffin was astonished. "Kev, you lucky, lucky bugger. What a catch!" Flopping about in the bottom of the boat was the slippery brown and white dapple of a small turbot. And Keen Kev had the rare feeling of a warm glow – happiness.

Gulls cried. "Go on, have another try," said Griffin. He agonised, trying to cram a nutshell, struggling for a timeline.

Emphatically, Keen Kev got embroiled when he had spied Delvin and some woman wearing a brown fedora. A similar hat had been Mel's sudden loss at the bring-and-buy stall. Coincidence? Unlikely. Turned peeping Tom, Keen

Kev took compromising photos that had since been bullied out of him by Margie.

Once more Griffin had the need to pinch himself.

There were images of Daphne Mudworth and Larry Biggot, Barri and Bridey, Barri and Joy! And … George!

Whatever tangent his thought processes took him Griffin repeatedly returned to George. The stupid Buttercup fiasco was firmly the fault of George and Rupert. What a pair of dumbos.

Margie was liable to cause chaos. Her error was thinking Keen Kev was loaded. Common sense said he couldn't be. Snickworthy and nearby villages had paltry client potential. It'd be different if he had inherited wealth. Of course! Keen Kev said Margie had found a "genie-whazzit" and had visited his gran – a Bunt. The gran was the link back to the Snooks – had to be.

"Kev, you said you were orphaned."

"Yeah, when I was ten. Dad was the Belters' wicketkeeper. Bet you didn't know that? But he had farm accident and mum died not long after."

"Whereabouts?"

"Australia."

"What? … I'm sorry. They went to Australia without you?"

"They just upped sticks. My gran said they had to leave sharpish, like."

"Why? Had something happened?"

"Dunno really. I think about it sometimes. It was when Sir Robert's wife got killed and we lived in a cottage that had rats and an earth floor that got knocked down. Dad used to shoot the rats with an airgun. The Mudworth bungalow's there now."

"Hmm. That was built in nineteen-fifty. Think I'll have a chat with Larry Biggot. He's been around forever and might be able to shed light on untoward dealings. Given your photo he might actually be helpful. Kev, you're going to have to nick those photos back from Margie. Kev!"

The *Pertelote* had begun to rock. And Keen Kev wasn't listening. Instead, he wrestled with his reel, his rod bending alarmingly.

"Hey, hey, hey, sit down, you goon. You'll have us over. What did you put on the hook?"

"A mackerel."

"A whole one? Jesus! Whatever's down there thinks it's Sainsbury's." Griffin chucked his roll-up into the sea. "Hand me your rod … HAND ME YOUR ROD!" He was up for a fight.

Seawater sloshing over the gunwales preceded a monster. Bop. Griffin cudgelled a stunning blow. The writhing ceased. "Blimey, Kev. First a turbot, now a conger eel. You should seriously think about turning professional. Tell me straight. Why did you brain the hunky punk?"

Enchanted by sun spangles on the water Keen Kev became pensive. "I wanted to buy a gold bracelet with the compensation money. Margie said she'd love me forever." He rubbed the corner of his eye with a salty finger.

Griffin ran a hand across his brow subconsciously ironing out the furrows. He felt a headache coming on. "Know what, Kev? Margie will think a bracelet's prettier than the turbot and she has ambition bigger than the conger. I suggest you sleep on my sofa until the storm blows over. But you must get the photos back."

Nodding agreement Keen Kev restrained himself to dangling a small slither of bait.

Up until the 'accident', both Larry Biggot and Ted Furet had been Belters. Afterwards, Sir Robert treated them in similar fashion. That was years ago.

Now, his bicycle leant against a blowth-white hawthorn hedge Larry, police tunic unbuttoned, sat alone on the bank downstream from the cricket pitch – the spot thirty years ago where he had worked things out and done nothing but give a warning. That was his way – the least amount of ripples.

The means 'how' continued to trundle around in broad daylight. The motive though had eluded him. A poor excuse, he knew, when there had been a murder. It was ironic to have brushed his uniform of sawdust after his "little chat" at Griffin the carpenter's. Because now everything was crystal clear as the stream itself.

Supposed to be on duty he, instead, listened to the water burble as it eddied over pebbles and around stones where a rapacious stickleback gorged and a brown trout swam in and out of shadow.

Shredding the Polaroid he threw the pieces one by one into the water and watched as the current bore them away from Snickworthy to the sea. Furet was a 'black mark' on the Belters like his dad Ted; though Ted was a real 'bad'un'.

But Ted was dead. Just as well. They could have hanged him. On raising the alarm with "Thar's bin a daft accident on the Steep," Ted had chugged off on Sir Robert's tractor.

Hitched, the short log trailer lurched as Larry arrived at the scene knackered – the only officer in attendance – having pedalled like a maniac, he jogged his bike the last hundred yards up the Steep. The prang had occurred on a blind bend by a field gate. Ted and his mother-in law had begun to wrestle the stag onto the trailer bed. "You was quick. Stupid, aint' it? Poor lady. We want to get this bleddy beast out of the way for you, Larry boy," Ted had said.

"Leave it where it is. I don't think evidence should be tampered with," Larry had said. Not yet wondering why Bindy Bunt had suddenly happened to be present.

Ted became rattled. "Evidence? Bain't it obvious what's happened? The stag was on the bonnet. You can see the gurt dent."

Larry checked, anyway.

The first dead body he'd seen, Lady Rosemary's was still warm, a broken antler stuck in her neck. Nasty. The stag, an insipid specimen long past rut success, was cold. Sawdust traces on its mangy coat were probably from Ted trying to get it into the trailer. Although the front legs and chest were smashed, a deep wound high on its neck was odd given it was supposedly struck by a low-slung sport car. And the amount of blood seemed disproportionate as if it had been splashed on. Suspicious.

He questioned if Sir Robert knew Ted was using the tractor and trailer. The reply was non-committal. "I work for him don't I?"

"Stay put," he had ordered before freewheeling back to the village for help.

Of course, the stag disappeared. And Ted was all innocence. "Stay put? Is that what yer said, young Larry? Thought yer said 'stew pot'."

Case closed, Larry was left brooding with reservations. The stag was poached, he deduced. Shot most likely, given the neck wound. The sawdust on the stag's coat did, indeed, come from the trailer. That was how the stag got to be where he found it. Obviously, the trailer and stag were hidden through the gate. Then it was evidently a waiting game. The stag was intended to halt the car, which it succeeded in doing. Lady Rosemary was then set upon and stabbed with the antler broken off from the stag's head.

Logically, Ted had to have needed a pair of accomplices. Firstly, someone must have warned that Lady Rosemary's car was approaching. Fired a gunshot, maybe? That was Edna, quite possibly. Then someone had to help drag the stag off the trailer and lay it across the car bonnet to stage a plausible accident. Here, he hazarded a guess at Bindy. But either way, what about the smashed windscreen, damage to the bodywork and injuries to the stag? Easy. A lump hammer.

It had not needed a genius to work it out. But why had Lady Rosemary been killed? That was what Larry could not fathom.

He had paid Ted a visit. "Didn't kill her nor the stag neither, honest to goodness," Ted had said. Next day Ted and Edna had done a bunk leaving behind a cage of ferrets and young Keen Kev. The Furet hovel got demolished. Bindy Bunt made some money. The bungalow got built. And Larry's problems soon escalated.

Ostracised by Sir Robert for "flagrant ineptitude" he, like Ted, never played another game for the Belters. Brockcombe later allowed him a handful of outings but in the end he simply made his excuses.

A dishwasher – a pied wagtail – alighted on a stone and bobbed its white breast. "Tu-reep, tu-reep."

"Quite right, bird. To reap what we sow."

Well, perhaps, Ted hadn't done in Lady Rosemary after all. It would do no harm to follow Griffin's advice, and pedal to Flawbridge and investigate a centuries old chip on a shoulder.

But what *was* he to do on a personal level? His dewlap was now bigger than a bullfrog's. And he continued to behave like a randy teenager despite life going pear-shaped – rapidly so. Being snapped at the love-nest was tantamount to making Daphne and him laughingstocks. Worse, since breaking-up with Gilly Criddle's lad, Margie's demands pauperised him. No end in sight there, either. In fact, Margie's marriage was a mere intermission, like ice cream at the Plaza.

The cost of buying and keeping the nag was unbelievable. The way Sir Robert had treated him made stealing the pheasant poults from the hen house – selflessly done for Daphne's sake – all the easier. That act alone should have seen him drummed out of the force.

However, Sir Robert did receive those brown envelopes accommodating the rent for Bondi's early stabling. Used towards his wine bill, it was the money Dapling paid for the stolen pheasants. That was the reality. Larry didn't think it too big a crime – the money, as long as it lasted, had simply boomeranged as Sir Robert bought the pheasants in the first place. Larry chuckled at the humour of it.

And now Prudence pestered him why there were never any tomatoes on his greenhouse plants and doubted the disappearance of leaves was down to slugs. Shutting Margie up, however, had been imperative.

Moreover, keeping the affair secret from Prudence and Tristan had worn him and Daphne to a frazzle.

Could things get any worse? Well yes, actually they could. He admonished himself for even thinking about arranging a theft of Bridey's wild strawberry Wedgwood.

Margie seemed as insatiable as the stickleback. But enough. Even of the wacky baccy. The cat was out of the bag. No, two cats were out of two bags.

TWENTY-FIVE

Hot Matches

Left to his own devices Flirty Bertie caused the log shed bats to reach the end of their tether as Big Doug, anaesthetised against his back's agony, snored away another hangover induced by Rupert's compassion. Slumber bucked the trend amid the morning activity.

Scratching Wellard's neck to kindle contented snuffle-snorts Mel, puffy black rings under her eyes, counted the hours. Less than seventy-two remained until the first ball was due to be bowled. Would the whiplash ease? Even if it didn't she had to play. Mind over matter. She imagined herself supported by sticks like a scarecrow.

The effect of the Belter's unexpected injuries was clear. The pig's felicity was in serious risk of truncation. Having heaved open the lid of the iron-banded church chest, Delvin took out the fusty flag of Saint George and considered flying it at half-mast.

At Nettlegot Joy struggled to find a skirt that fitted before she hurried to the lock-up for the morning papers prior to preparing breakfast.

The weekly rag with its piece by Vera Scragg beside the toast rack, Sir Robert's boiled eggs suffered violence similar to the hunky punk. George and Henry spontaneously found they had things to do. Their respective lists avoided the gaping hole in the damp billiard room ceiling where wattle and lath were visible after the collapse of ornate plaster.

"Excuse me, Pater. Must go and yank the self-seeded buddleias out of our walls," sighed George, making the task seem imperative. He whistled Lobb the Duckdog from under the table as an additional act of mercy. It occurred to Henry that checking for any forwarded mail was not a bad idea, either.

Before rubbing down the sweat lather on Bondi's flanks Margie lifted the third straw bale on the left and shrieked with fury. The sandwich bag of photos had vanished from the stable during her ride. Furet had ferreted.

In a safe corner away from sawdust and wood shaving flames flared in Griffin's ashtray. Prior to him striking the match Griffin had thought Larry exceedingly forthcoming. Beans had been spilt.

A dusty rucksack and assorted suitcases were hastily packed in differing Snickworthy abodes.

On the warpath Margie found herself 'home' alone. So, too, did Mrs Biggot and Tristan Mudworth. With Rupert promising total confidence Larry and Daphne had withdrawn to the Stump's upstairs to share the 'Bridal Suite' with a desiccated bee and mummified flies until something more permanent could be sorted.

Below them, a beer tap gurgled and spat taxing froth.

Holding up the lunchtime bar Jerzy greeted George and Henry with a smoke ring and settled to discuss serious matters. Polish pheasants, Jerzy believed, were possibilities for the hen house – and a welcome distraction to the enormities of the cricket match. A letter neatly folded in his Barbour pocket had given Henry the green light. The stone barn had passed muster for conversion.

"Goes without saying Henry will need some high security," offered George. "May I venture the services of Nettlegot Ned?"

"Neither of you are taking me seriously," said Henry.

"Yes, we are," responded Jerzy. "Look, bung straw into the campervan and that'll do nicely for your Cuckoo Marans. I've said you can have that wreck."

Henry looked a little downcast. "You also convinced me it had character. As each day goes by I'm realising the folly of 'Folly Farmyard'."

"Buck up," said George. "It's a wonderful name. Remember no more Jubilee Line. No more city smuts in your beak. Just Zum air."

"If you're dreaming of forming a shoot you won't find Bazanties in that book of yours, Henry," advised Jerzy. "Mum, however, says Dad once swore by them. They're stay at homes. White neck rings like common parsons but they're smaller, and more willing to flush and die than Old English Blacknecks. Those tend to sensibly keep their heads down. Plump for the Polish any day to add spark to a posh sod's gun. No offence, George … or you Henry."

"Wish we had a gun bowler," said George, changing tack quickly to the pressing issue. "There's no way Big Doug blunderbuss is able to play. So tough on Mel, and such rotten luck. As we can't lay hands on a 'Purdey' it's going to be down to you, Henry … and Delvin's tweakers. Course, I'll do my best, but what about you, Jerzy? Fancy a bowl on Saturday?"

"Risk getting the blame for years to come? I don't think so. I'll do my best top of the order. After that I'm diving for the bunkers with my rabbit's foot. But it might be better if it was a rat's. We've got a hellish long tail. And there're rabbits attached."

Henry regarded George closely. "Are you really drafting in Timmy *and* Keen Kev?"

"Ta-daaah," said Bridey finished changing the barrel and emerging through the trapdoor behind the bar.

"Hello, Houdini," said Henry, suavely.

Jerzy puffed another smoke ring and slapped Henry hard on the shoulder. "Best you know, Brides, from today Henry will have to learn to belsh his chilvers. He's officially ditched a muddy-want life in London's underground to farm Zum soil."

"Ooh sir, 'ow are yer yeows?" Bridey gave Henry a curtsy having already pinched her cheeks on the way up from the cellar. She laughed at Henry's puzzlement. "I'm asking after yer ewes … lady sheep, city boy."

"Hadn't you better question his seed quality?" quipped Jerzy, lasciviously.

To Bridey it was water off a duck's back. Henry, however, calculated a response.

"Bridey, can you go and find me a tissue?" She handed him a box from under the bar. "Lovely. Thank you. Jerzy, can I have a puff of your fag?"

"Course."

Taking the cigarette Henry inspected the filter, put it to his lips and, from one inhalation, blew three smoke rings spitting through each with a single gobbet. His performance over in seconds, Henry handed back the cigarette. "That, Jerzy, is a result of education – Hellfire Club, Cambridge University. Now apologise to Bridey, there's a good chap."

Jerzy mumbled sorriness into his half-empty pint and Henry went to wipe the floor.

"Wow," breathed George.

"Couldn't help overhear you needin' a ... whatwazzit ... a thingy bowler," said Bridey letting go of the bar, certain it had prevented her from swooning. "Think I can help yer. I can get hold of a bloke for the Belters. He's rapid. Yer've played against him a while back, George. And he'd come recommended by that copper whatizname."

"You mean Larry Biggot? You sure?" George queried.

"Sure I'm sure. Thinks the sun shines out of Ollie's arse, he does. Said so in me front room."

"Ollie who, Bridey?"

"Ollie Wardle, Pol's bloke. Yer must remember Pol. Any road, she still remembers you. Wants to plant yer a rose garden at your place, she says. Ollie's the bloke Big Doug tonked in ter the goblin's gob ... I mean Ollie bowled the ball that ... Yer okay, George? Yer've gone a funny colour."

"Polly," George muttered. "Polly," he repeated. "It *was* her I saw." He seemed to descend into reverie, somewhere misty and faraway.

"Still with us, George?" said Jerzy back on form. "Cor, Wardle. What a legend. Single-handedly annihilated us. Looked like he'd fallen out of the 'Rocky Horror Picture Show'. Took out my middle stump. Nothing I could do. Too quick. He's a gun bowler, no mistake." He suddenly became serious. "How does Biggot know him, Bridey? And anyway what's he doing in your house?"

"Have a care, Jerzy," said Henry.

"S'alright, Henry." She touched his hand fleetingly and gently. "Ask the copper yerself. Jerzy." She pointed a finger at the beams. "He's upstairs."

"Doing what?" Jerzy burst out.

"Me lips are sealed," said Bridey, catching Rupert's eye as he entered the bar.

"So ... do I ask Ollie or not?"

"Definitely," said Jerzy "I speak on behalf of my captain who's ... still miles away." He gave George a nudge.

"Uh?" George seemed mazed.

"Great. Ta, Jerzy" said Bridey. "I'll give Pol a tinkle once I've picked Lili up from yer mam's. Gilly's so wonderful wiv her. Best babysitter in the world.

Good as a gran to Lili."

Jerzy joined George in looking mazed.

The phone rang and Rupert picked up. "Burning Stump ... Hi, Joy .... Surprise guest out of the blue to see George ... okay ... Round the Belters up ... What? Including Keen Kev? ... Team meeting, billiard room, six o'clock ... Absolutely not. Can't blame Sir Robert for insisting ... Okey-doke ... I'll pass the message on to the reprobates ... Bye."

Catching the gist of the conversation, Bridey had a question. "If I can get Ollie over here for this evening, does he need to dress up?"

"Ollie? Whom exactly are we talking about?" It was Rupert who rapidly needed to get up to speed.

Blaring The Clash's 'Death or Glory' and drowning out the year's first cuckoo, at five fifty-seven, the white van of 'Brockcombe Garden Services' scrunched to a standstill on Nettlegot's patchy gravel and beeped. Aiming towards the grand oaken front door, Mel, hands in pockets, gingerly turned her neck.

Ollie leaned grinning out of the window. "Hiya! You're the blacksmiff, right?"

Recognition dawning Mel grinned back. "And you're Mr Nine-for-Eight. I remember. I nearly hit you for six." She guffawed. "Gawd, you look like a sea urchin."

"My hair? These spikes took me an hour. Bridey said I had to try making a good impression. See, clean white shirt."

There was no time for Mel to also say she admired Ollie's earring. Lobb the Duckdog careered around the corner, tongue lolling and with an idiot grin. A plump dachshund yapped in surprisingly fast pursuit.

"Porthos! Oohoo. Oohoo." Hastening into sight trotted a buxom woman in her sixties clad in country tweeds. A monocle attached to a piece of string around her neck bumped against her chest, and she held a pair of secateurs.

"Brakes!" she said coming to a halt in front of Mel and twinkling an intelligent eye. A black leather patch covered her other. "No need to catch flies, dear. Sorry. I sound like a demented owl. Never could learn to whistle." The good eye scrutinised. "You have to be the famous young, iron-banging, pig lady Robert warned me about. The Belters always have been rather an eclectic bunch. Buggered your neck, I hear."

Mel smiled. She liked this strange galleon. "Hazards of ducks. It is feeling a bit easier, thank you, Mrs ..."

"You can call me Frances."

Deciding to be sociable Ollie got out of the van to introduce himself. Aunt Frances needed a fraction of a second to gather her wits. "Oh gosh. It's Attila the Hun. Whatever next? Go round to the French windows both of you.

They're open. The vicar and a rough, scar-faced individual are already mingling. So is that nice man wearing a cravat – another house guest braving it, I'm led to believe, and lending George moral support. And there's a quite ghastly object amongst the exhibits on the billiard table. No prizes for guessing Robert's foot tapping and obstreperous." The yaps became audible again. "Ah. Must tackle my dog and Robert's canine mishap. Any more circuits and they'll end up thin as rakes. I'll be back. I've words to say to you cricketers."

No sooner had Aunt Frances' hoots faded than the vroom of Buttercup heralded the arrival of Rupert, Old Willy and a box of claret. Almost bumper-to-bumper came a Griffin-driven Bumpkin delivering Big Doug, Jerzy, and a whimpering Keen Kev. "Stop your mither, Kev," said Big Doug. "You're doing a noble deed in part penance. And it's hardly likely Sir Robert will have you hanged, drawn and a quartered in front of his surprise guest."

Forces joined, Big Doug hobbled in his own discomfort – a pain that swelled outside the French windows as he saw tortoises Hobbs and Hammond being the focus of an inquisitive Wickham.

Keen Kev, on the other hand, seemed to perk up being party to Ollie's welcome. "Guts for garters! Who invited this oik to my house?" exploded Sir Robert.

It was Jerzy's cue to fidget.

Claret bottles clinked. "That was me," said Rupert, putting his peace offering on the billiard table to keep company with a brown hat, a Dictaphone, the week's newspaper and the notorious hunky punk head. If he grimaced he hid it well. "May I present Douglas Birchtree's replacement for tomorrow, Mr Ollie Wardle, scourge of Quantock batsmen."

The senior Wimble-Clatt was uncharitable. "Scares them to death, most like."

"Took nine for eight against us on day of the hunky punk, if you recall. Looks a trifle bohemian, I admit, but best bowling average in these parts for fifty years."

Sir Robert grunted begrudgingly.

"And he's volunteering to save Belter pride and Mel's pig," said Rupert.

"In return for the family silver, I'd hazard a guess."

"Bog off," said Ollie finding his voice.

Belter jaws went slack. Sir Robert turned puce. For some unbeknown reason George gave a self-satisfied smirk quite out of character that quickly vanished as he caught Keen Kev's eye. Outside arose frenzied yapping and a pheasant's startled alarm.

"Wickham!" uttered George, a picture of concern.

Sudden clapping broke the tension. A panting Porthos struggling under an arm and Lobb the Duckdog to heel, Aunt Frances had sailed into the room. "That was a rebuke fully deserved, Robert. Aren't you going to introduce me to everyone?"

Sir Robert fought for air.

"I see I shall have to do it myself, as always." She laughed a deep belly laugh. "I'm Frances. And I show up when needed – like Mary Poppins. Why am I needed? Well, I shall enlighten you." She popped Porthos on the floor and tapped the dog on the nose. "You, leave fezzies alone." Then she took an envelope from her skirt.

"Heaven preserve me, another bloody letter," said Sir Robert.

"Quite correct, Robert. This is one sent to me by Mrs Bobowski. In it she demands I send her a cheque for one thousand pounds otherwise she threatens to write to the Queen of Denmark to say I was complicit in a kidnap. Outrageous."

"That's Margie for you," said Jerzy not sounding the least bit surprised.

"Really? I've no intention of paying her a penny. Enlighten me as to what prompted her to think I would." said Aunt Frances putting Jerzy on the spot. He could only shrug.

Aunt Frances cast her eye around the billiard room. "Anybody? No? Oh, pull your socks up."

Rupert raised a digit, umpire fashion. "Me, again, I'm afraid. I knew how much Jerzy – Mr Bobowski – wanted to watch the vital game in Nottingham the day after our overnight stay with you. Had I not taken measures he would have been forced to miss it. 'Fraid things backfired a bit."

The eye twinkled. "I've had a word or two with George about your small error of judgement." George smiled weakly, still getting over the fact that Aunt Frances was actual flesh and blood.

Wanting his own judgement put on record Keen Kev piped up. "Margie Bobowski said way back that I'm related to the Wimble-Clatts."

"And so is everybody if we return to the bare skinned aquatic ape," Aunt Frances snapped. "I detect this awful young lady's become the bane of village life. Coincides with Nettlegot going to wrack and ruin. Why is that? What I've seen of her I don't think there's anything to be frightened of."

"But you're the one with the war medal," muttered George quietly enough so as not to interrupt. Jerzy had to bite on a knuckle to control himself, but was unable to contain a splutter. Aunt Frances gave him a withering look.

"You're a feckless bunch of namby-pambies," she professed. "However, not everyone is cut from the same cloth. There are maybe one or two exceptions I can see, who realise Mrs Bobowski's just a headstrong filly that needs breaking-in."

Good luck with that, thought Jerzy.

"Well, I want nothing to do with her," said Mel, leaning against the empty trophy cabinet at the back of the billiard room. "Hold on." Suddenly intrigued by the brown hat, she wandered across to inspect it. "Hey, this is my fedora!" she exclaimed

"Sorry Mel, it's actually mine," said Joy, cutting short her relay of mugs and tea. "I had to recover it from the bring-and-buy. Couldn't have Kev seeing it and making a connection to Nettlegot or jumping to wrong conclusions. More fool me. I shoved it in a cupboard only for George to unearth it rummaging for things to box up for the jumble.

"Absolutely," said George. "I was out so early that morning that nobody saw me drop the box off at the stall. Joy was livid when I told her where the hat had gone. She said she didn't want anyone knowing she'd been down to the stone barn."

"That's my new home," said Henry, thoroughly pleased with his day so far.

Big Doug made it even better. "I hear via George you're looking for a caravan to live in while you renovate. I've just the girl, if you don't mind blackcurrant berry motif patterned wallpaper and a chemical loo. Her name's Angela ... Sorry George, you were talking about a hat."

"I was." Casting knowing glances at Joy and Barri, George tapped the side of his nose with his finger. "I didn't ask questions. I simply went to retrieve the hat but found Mel already wearing it. So I suggested to Joy that I should go on a false errand and have the Land Rover break down. Then it couldn't have been me who left the box. Meaning no link between the hat and Nettlegot."

"The mouse in the exhaust," said Jerzy, commendably keeping up.

"Mad as a bag of frogs," muttered Old Willy.

Again forgetting his place, Keen Kev started and pointed a wavering finger at Joy. "Then it was *you* the vicar groped!"

"I'm not in the habit of groping anyone," said Delvin irritably. "Like the other items, the hat is on the table for good reason – my decision. This charade has to stop right now. Joy, put down those mugs and come here." He beckoned her to him. She did as bade and stared down at her shoes. Sir Robert looked uncomfortable and began to fuss over Lobb the Duckdog.

Delvin took a deep breath. "Quite the sea fisherman, aren't you, Kevin. I've heard all you said on *Pertelote*. The tape was very atmospheric. I especially liked the slop of waves and the plaintive gull cries ... You silly, silly man. The lunchtime you played Clouseau, I wasn't groping Joy, I was hugging her after she had told me something. And I was quite entitled to." He took a deeper breath. "Joy is my daughter."

A hush descended in an instant, making the sound from outside the French windows of Wickham's beak tapping on Hammond's shell sound like gunshots.

"Oh my," said Rupert, finally.

"Now I look at the dimpled chins ..." observed Mel, head cocked to one side.

"Mel, shut up for once," Rupert hissed.

"Dang I," said Old Willy, eyes fixed on the hole in the ceiling. "Turned me back for a minute and this place has gorn all to lippets."

It was left to Griffin to ask the bolder question. "Why did you have to meet at the stone barn? Why not just in the church or rectory?"

Delvin's reply was immediate. "And have Kenneth just turn up? How ironic life can be."

"But why the secrecy for so long?"

Delvin gripped Joy's hand in his. "Do I have your permission?" he asked her quietly. Her squeeze of assent was hard to discern.

"For Joy's sake, I didn't want a scandal – something untold I couldn't possibly share with either the village or the bishop. And now it seems so very stupid. Joy's mother – Olivia – and I met at the Giant's Causeway. I was a grockle and I stumbled across her. She had her nose in a book of Yeats' poetry and fingers in a bag of ginger nuts. I had a dog collar, a bottle of fizzy pop and the cheek to say hello." Delvin composed himself. "The result turned out to be Joy. Olivia was Catholic. Of course I was C. of E. We could never marry because of our differences in interpreting wafers and wine. When the Troubles began I was a barracks' chaplain and things became very difficult … and Olivia shouldn't have been where she was …" His voice tailed away.

Joy's dimpled chin quivered. "It's okay, Dad," she said and picked up the sorry tale where he had left off. "Mum wanted to talk to Dad about me. I had never wanted to talk to him. I never understood daft principles. Dad got a message to Mum saying he'd found a safe place to meet – a quiet bar but his side of the peace wall. Mum was then killed by a bomb … Barri, say something."

The Welshman's eyes were watering. "I … You and your Da never said she was one of the ones in there. Cach! Does what the world thinks matter so much?" He ground his teeth in sudden anger. "Permission to drag Furet outside and beat the crap out of him."

Keen Kev squeaked.

"Permission denied. The Belters need him to play cricket, so George tells me," said Delvin, more his usual self.

"Wretched ducklings," bemoaned Big Doug.

"Indeed," Delvin agreed. Fighting his inner demons his lack of support for Keen Kev was understandable. "Anyway, what I believe my daughter would like Barri to admit is that he was also present at the damned blast. His scar is because of it. He ignored his injuries to help amongst the carnage. Bravest, kindest bastard it's ever been my privilege to encounter, I thought at the time." The expression on Barri's face had a subtle change of discomfort. Delvin seemed to have satisfaction seeing it. "But let it be known," he added, "none of us three would be in Snickworthy without Sir Robert's generosity of spirit."

Absorbed in tickling Lobb the Duckdog's tummy, Sir Robert chose his words carefully. "Both the Reverend and I have lost those whom we loved." Keen Kev squeaked, again, and found Griffin move to stand beside him and surreptitiously kick his ankle. "I retain a network of old school chums," explained Sir Robert, "some of whom happened to be in the army. As it was, George and I needed a home help. The cricket pitch needed attending to. And the church needed a vicar who wasn't bothersome. Which is why there is absolutely no cause for the bishop to discover any improprieties ... Do I make myself clear, Mr Furet?"

Keen Kev nodded his head so furiously that it was in danger of emulating the hunky punk's.

"Nice to see you being firm Robert," said Aunt Francis. "But we appear to be left with the problems of the press and the church adornment. Don't worry about Xavier, I'll deal with him after you've played your match."

"Xavier?" queried Sir Robert.

"The bishop. He and I suffered the same governess."

Eminently aware of the potential for her own suffering and loss Mel had something to add. "Can we possibly know the team for Saturday?"

"See for yourself," said George, handing her list of names scribbled on the back of an old envelope. It read:

Team to play Pitchforkers
Jerzy
Barri
Mel
Henry
Griffin
Rupert
Me
Delvin
Willy
Wardle
Furet

"Is this open for discussion?" Mel asked.
After a curious glance at Keen Kev, George answered. "No."

TWENTY-SIX

Ifs and Butts

A gull stood to attention atop of the church flagpole. On a sublime morning without a scouting cloud, the cross of Saint George hung limp. The game was on.

Brushed clean of caking mud Wellard looked a smart pig as Mel, shaking a bucket of barley laced with harvested earthworms, encouraged him towards the cricket pitch where, with preparations almost complete, Barri advised Sir Robert.

"I done my best, but I don't fancy facing the new ball out there in the middle. Not long since the moles wore bathers. Pitch is still a tad tacky. Leather won't come on. Difficult. The Belters could do with batting second."

"We can only hope George wins the toss, then."

"Cach. I'm banking on the Pitchforkers not finding Snicky in the first place. But if they do I'm relying on our secret weapon." He tapped the side of his nose.

Both men leaned on one of the two steel bar pens, empty save for straw bales and water troughs, erected by Barri and George near the manor house boundary and which now awaited their occupants.

"Morning gentlemen," said Aunt Frances sipping a cup of tea and still in her dressing gown. "I've just seen Henry. Says George is lending him the Land Rover and he's off to Mr Birchtree to finalise the caravan. Wants to ensure there's room to hang an oar. I hope you're both focusing on the game ahead."

"Without question, m'dear. If we're going to outplay the Pitchforkers we can't be having any more distractions."

"Glad to hear it. I was just wondering, have either of you'd seen Porthos? He was with me before Joy bought me this cuppa."

She was interrupted by a loud shout from around the side of the house. "Come here, now!" There was a clatter of wings. And Wickham glided by pursued enthusiastically by Porthos and Lobb the Duckdog.

"How interesting. Lobb hasn't shown the least bit of interest in pheasants before," said Sir Robert. "Good dog, Lobb!" he hollered.

Halting briefly Lobb the Duckdog wagged a tail at its master before continuing to pelt after its small, rotund mentor that had no intention of slowing. George was losing ground, his shouts going unheeded.

Aunt Frances passed her cup and saucer to Barri, hitched up her dressing gown, and lent a fresh pair of legs. "Porthos! Oohoo, oohoo!" Passing the crockery to Sir Robert Barri set off, too.

For a species of bird often presumed to have little brain, Wickham bucked the trend. Beating wings for a kick of momentum it veered across the stream to the sanctuary of Nettlegot Ned. Porthos, in whom Lobb the Duckdog retained total faith, had yet to become acquainted. The dogs hit the water. One torpedoed across, the other splashed. Nettlegot Ned prepared to face incursion.

Inside the house Joy put down the phone and walked purposefully to the French windows. "Sir Robert! Ah, there you are. That Radley chap just rang. The Pitchforkers plus one bull are on their way ... Where is everyone?"

Before Sir Robert could reply the phone rang again. Off Joy scurried to hear Mrs Dapling reporting Timmy being in bed with a rash. The Belters had no twelfth man.

"Blue or purple for the pig?" asked Ollie holding up two tubes of hair dye.

"Purple," said Polly, snuggle-tousled from sleep, her nose poking over the top of the duvet. "It's special. Means good judgement and supportive – perfect choice for today. Blue's peace and order. No chance of that."

At Griffin's place Keen Kev was also rousing, but he was more tousled than snuggled, stiff after a third night on the sofa. He, too, had a pressing decision to make – whether or not to run the gauntlet to get his cricket bag out of Bramble Cottage. Hesitating to decide he implored Griffin's opinion.

"Remember what Frances said, Margie's nothing to be afraid of," Griffin ventured, finding his eyes had begun to itch.

Keen Kev flicked his squirrel tail at a moth. "Then, perhaps, Frances can collect my kitbag."

"Goodness sake, grow some balls. If it makes you feel better I'll come with you. How's that? We'll swing by the paddock on the way. If the horse isn't there Margie'll be on her ride, anyway."

Ken Kev blew out his cheeks with relief. "Ta. Have you seen my key?"

"It's where you last left it. Hang on, there's someone at the door."

It was Larry Biggot. "Strange turn of events. Thought I'd come and tell you. I visited that address you gave me in Flawbridge. It was a shit pit, but an empty one. I spoke to neighbours. The Bunt woman's buggered off it seems, and left no forwarding address."

Flappy-eared, Keen Kev overheard. He lay back down in the foetus position on the sofa feeling the panic of being alone in the world and glad of Griffin's company.

"Well, I should go and find Daphne," said Larry taking his leave.

Griffin had one last thought. "Why don't you two come to the match this afternoon? There's no point you hiding anymore. The bush telegraph's hotter than Dante's Inferno."

Larry was evidently shocked. Whether it was from the invitation or a sudden awareness of the gossip only he knew.

Intact save for a trifling tail feather Wickham perched on the heavy roller and blinked relief. Nose tapped but still panting from the excitement, Porthos, too, was remarkably unscathed. That this was so was down to Barri. The Belters' injury list, however, had just grown. Barri could move his fingers okay but his thumb throbbed like billy-o and was turning what was proving to be the colour of the day.

After a rough inspection Frances was consoling. "Don't think it's broken."

Barri sighed ruefully, mesmerised by the swelling. "The ruddy ram packs a wallop, doesn't it? Hope I'll be able to bat. There's no way I can keep to Ollie's rockets. Griffin will have to wicky."

The new information seemed to totally bypass George. "You were amazing. Porthos' rescue was worthy of 'Twickers'," he enthused, passing mention of Twickenham, the home of English rugby.

Things had happened in a blur. With wet shoes and socks he and Barri had vaulted the post and rail. He recalled Lobb the Duckdog cowering low to the rear of two molehills, reliving a personal nightmare, when Nettlegot Ned had charged. Commendably, the dachshund had stood its ground, yapping, having changed sport from pheasant chasing. There could only have been one outcome for the novice had Barri not spontaneously intervened. On the run and in a fluidity of movement he had picked up Porthos and delivered the perfect swift pass to George before being late tackled.

"Keep your Twickers, I was thinking Cardiff Arms Park," said Barri. "I'm rusty though. Didn't manage the sidestep."

"What hell else can go wrong?" wondered George.

The answer involved a cuckoo having found a nest.

Keen Kev and Griffin stood outside Bramble Cottage, the key useless. The front door had been bolted from within. "Groovy. It's like Fort Knox. If you had another brain cell you'd be a plant. Didn't you even think to take the back door key?" said Griffin exasperated, drawing on a roll-up.

The reply had a tone of helplessness and dejection. "Never used to lock it. Why should I?"

"The reason, Kev, is currently clopping the Quantocks." Griffin had a nasty feeling of yet more messy entanglement. He had to confess being partly culpable. "So are you going to borrow kit or do you want me to break a window?"

Keen Kev hopped from foot to foot. His squeak drowned by the sudden sneeze.

"Hay fever," sniffled Griffin.

TWENTY-SEVEN

Shell Shocked

Rumpled Belters gathered short in number and motley attired. Balancing an armful of clobber Keen Kev had succeeded in raiding pickings from the fetid depths of the Nettlegot kit cupboard. "George, can I borrow these? Joy thinks I can."

"Then why ask me?" said George flippantly, without properly looking around. Had he bothered he would have recognised his cast-off greying whites and cumbersome old cricket boots. Then there were the mildewed cotton-coated batting pads, the perished rubber spiked gloves, and an ancient bat, the string of its handle grip unravelling and brittle. Each item was marked 'A W-C'. "No sign of Henry, yet; nor that Wardle character," whinged George.

"Patience," said Jerzy. "Dead sure Henry won't be long. It's been ten minutes since he passed us towing the caravan to … his barn. Your Land Rover needs seeing to by the way. The blue smoke wasn't good. Dunno about Ollie. Your grotty dad might have put him off. But I've got my fingers crossed he'll turn up."

"Really?" said George sounding peeved.

A truck's crashing gearbox gave an inkling the Pitchforker's arrival was imminent. They were early. The church clock was yet to strike the half hour.

"There's still our secret weapon," muttered Barri to no one in particular, and "Ow" as he tried on his batting glove.

"Garn, you lot don't half live in a warren," Radley hailed in greeting. "Where's trouble?" Fixing his gaze on the group of Belters he spied Mel. "There she be! Billy boy, go and say hello."

Leaping from the truck Billy beamed from ear to ear. "Hiya, gorgeous," he said.

"Ahem." Sir Robert hobbled forward from the front door and held out a hand to Radley. "Welcome to Nettlegot. Sir Robert Wimble-Clatt. You're more than punctual."

Being civil Radley shook Sir Robert's hand. "Radley, sir. We would have been earlier but Hairy Fred played silly buggers. First day trip of his life and he's got less room than he should 'cos we need space for the pig. Best get him out. Pity he can't see the scenery – 'tis praper job." Over his shoulder his Pitchforkers all wearing blazers and ties, with a large shaggy exception, had a stretch. A mix of youth and experience they tended to lean towards the latter and included Ken, the landlord from the Lion who practised a quick bowling action.

"Hey, look at him. An old-stager in his dotage," said Barri braving an early sledge.

"We're going to be fine, lads," said Radley in quick retort. "This lot look as if they've gone AWOL from a field hospital."

"So do you," thought Mel. Studying Radley, he appeared gaunt and paler than she remembered. Billy, however, who had lowered the truck tailgate, seemed unchanged. "There, there, 'tis okay, fella." He said softly, pulling on Hairy Fred's halter. "Come and meet Wellard." After a few staggers, the shaggy blind bull let himself be led without complaint. "Please guide us in the right direction, Miss Mel." The flush in her cheeks and bobbed curtsy were worthy of Bridey. With the stakes so high she had cut it fine – her neck felt easier.

Intent on gouging his peepers out with his fists Griffin got a nudge. "Is this really happening?" asked George.

"Suppose so," said Griffin having made himself boggle-eyed. "Can't see just at the mo. The pollen's awful."

"You sure you're able to keep wicket?"

"Ask me again once I've put my head under a tap. Don't you think you ought to say hello, being our captain and all that?"

Radley clapped his hands. "Shall we get on? I think the umpires should be introduced. Herbert!" A small, wiry, silver-haired man of uncertain age stepped forward. A cigar poked from the breast pocket of his blazer.

Feeling the urge to swear George somehow managed to dilute his epithet. "Fiddlesticks," he ejaculated. "We appear to have made a slight oversight."

"Hur hur, blooming amateurs," taunted Radley. "Fair 'nough. Sort yourselves out while we go and get changed." He cast his eyes around the field of play. "Yer do have a pavilion?"

"Er, not exactly," said George. "We've a billiard room that serves for both teams.

"Beg pardon?" The look on Radley's face was inscrutable.

"Excuse me a sec," said George, "I must have a quick word with our vicar." Delvin found himself hauled aside. Flustered, George whispered, "Can your divine guidance find us an umpire, pronto?"

God's beneficence was instant. Vaulting the stile was Henry. Clambering after him came Bridey, Lili and, ever so carefully, Big Doug. The sense of relief in George was profound.

He ushered to the Pitchforkers. "Right, if you'll all like to follow me. By the way, I'm George, the Belters captain."

"Ar," said Radley. "I was wonderin'."

Beep-beep, beep-beep-beep. A white van pulled up in Church Lane to Bridey's delight and set Lili showing-off doing roly-polies. "That must be the oik," Sir Robert reasoned. However, he was of lighter spirit. Thanks to Henry his bank balance had swelled to a far greater degree than Barri's thumb. Overall, however, it was merely an attractive rock pool beside his sea of debt.

❖ ❖ ❖

The open French windows offered an invitation. Wasps hummed at the semi-circular mesh food tents popped wisely over individual plates of strawberry jam and clotted cream-topped scones, assorted sandwiches, and Victoria sponges that rested on a large patterned tablecloth smoothed over the plywood rectangle protecting the billiard table's baize.

In a corner, surrounded by higgledy-piggledy cricket bags, their paraphernalia of content, and a jumble of strewn clothing, George fumbled with his pad buckles. Loose cotton folds of his baggy white trousers were proving a nuisance. Things had gone badly from the moment he lost the toss. Radley had put the Belters into bat without hesitation.

"Want some help, there?" Joy asked, feeling self-conscious and in sombre mood.

"No, I'm fine," George lied and gave a sigh. "We so need new blood."

"Given what's happening that's rather an unfortunate thing to say," Joy said. She cast a doughty glance through the French windows and winced. Never had she expected such a batting collapse. The instigator, the Pitchforkers amiable landlord, was a beast unleashed. Runs were hard to come by.

Putting himself down to bat at number seven George had thought himself fairly safe for an hour at least. He was wrong and took Dutch courage from knocking back fortifying slugs of apple brandy from Delvin's hip flask. Ken was sending down purlers with grunting effort and maximum effect. And the Belters' battered and bruised top and upper middle order were wilting despite Jerzy holding up an end.

Although Barri's thumb was mercifully unbroken by Nettlegot Ned, protecting it from further harm proved costly – a delivery that pitched and reared freakishly he lobbed to silly point. "Never ceases to astound what can be achieved between lunch and my pipe and slippers," Ken goaded as Barri trudged off, a warrior pained. The Belters would warrant a substitute fielder. But that was in due course.

In the here and now, trying to keep a steady neck and up the scoring rate, Mel had vainly swung from the hip. Switching tactics she hit straight with full meaty resonating clumps to twice disturb stream tiddlers before her middle stump was uprooted. As she sat on a bale inside Wellard's pen not bothering to take off her pads Hairy Fred snorted sympathy. "Hard cheddar, luv," Billy had said.

And after a further short passage of play a squawk of anguish signalled Henry's anticlimactic demise. Out ell bee, the ball thudding into his privates was surely too high. Herbert, though, raised a finger to remove a threat that was batting with a measure of bombast. Miffed, Henry went to socialise, seeking solace.

The dismissal of Griffin was simply tragic. He heard the death rattle as he sneezed. Perched on Sir Robert's shooting stick and wearing an umpire's coat that was far too tight, Big Doug despaired for Wellard.

"Rather falling apart at the seams," reflected Aunt Frances helping herself to a slice of Victoria sponge. Tail-waggers Porthos and Lobb the Duckdog were hopeful but Aunt Frances told it as it was.

On field cheers signalled an addition to the Belter procession.

Everything rode on George, and it gave him the collywobbles. His mind whirred for any reasonable excuse not to bat. The suspect breach-birth of a lamb in the top pasture, perhaps? Somewhat late in the month, but plausible. A fox amongst the India runners? Unlikely in broad daylight, and he would have to conjure up blood and feathers. Maybe, a buzzard stuck down a chimney? He was about plump for the lamb when Sir Robert poked his shock of white hair in from the outside sunshine. "Show some mettle. A captain's innings is needed. Carpe diem."

Spikes prudently shed, Rupert, the sacrificial lamb to a "yes, no, yes, oops" running disaster between the wickets, shuffled into the sanctuary of the billiard room in his socks and chucked his bat onto the soft landing of a Pitchforker blazer. "Sorry George, I just wanted to get off strike. Big Doug's crying real tears out there."

"Why? Empathy with Griffin?"

"Didn't you see? The moron gave me out. He's too honest. Want my advice? Get your head down. Death awaits the faint-hearted."

"Oh, God." George got to his feet. The laces of his cricket shoes were untied, and he wobbled – a problem Rupert easily diagnosed. "George, you're pissed."

"Not overly."

"Can't let you make a idiot of yourself, Belters honour's at stake." Rupert went down on one knee and did the necessary tying. "If that wretched bowler don't get you, Joy will happily murder you for wearing your spikes indoors." And seeing her flicking a tea towel at a wasp, added sonorously: "Will you not, Joy?"

"Without question," she replied, feigning anger.

Irrefutably a feeder, Aunt Frances took a moment's respite between scenes. "That nasty little umpire's looking this way and tapping his watch. George Wimble-Clatt, hurry up. At this rate Hobbs and Hammond could beat you to the crease."

Rupert shoved a much-taped, red-blemished bat in George's glove. "Go on George, tally-ho for heaven's sake. If a Pitchforker appeals, bet your life Herbert will time you out. You can't be another Heygate." Rupert had turned the leaves of his mental history book back to 1919 when Sussex had pootled to Taunton a player short. A suited spectator, Harold Heygate, was pressed into service. An ex-professional, but worse luck a crock – fourteen years since a first-class cricket game, interim war wounds and bad arthritis gave him the capability of Keen Kev.

With Somerset and Sussex scores level, the ninth Sussex wicket fell to cue hiatus. Poor Heygate. With pads strapped on top of his blue serge he made a valiant but fruitless attempt to reach the wicket from the Old Pavilion. After some minutes a Somerset stickler appealed. The umpire, a respected Test match official, ruled that Heygate was out and the game ended in an unhappy tie. From the position the Belters were in, to even think of running the Pitchforkers close was absurd.

A smattering of polite claps greeted George's overdue appearance. "Dazzy-snoo don't look viddy," mumbled Old Willy concerned at the Belter skipper's teetery state. The sun's glare caused George to squint as he dawdled to the crease. He adjusted his cricket cap while circumnavigating deck chairs, picnic baskets, and dogs tails, particularly one that was like an old fashion pump handle attached to a Staffy whose other end George found perturbing. "Wuff."

"Wedgy, behave." Bare legs spread out in front of her, a young lady in a floral print summer dress sitting on a tartan blanket rolled up a large scroll of paper.

An intoxicating memory of warm breath flooded George's being. "Polly?"

"Who did you think?"

George's cheeks flared involuntarily. "You've … changed your hairdo."

"Meeeeeh!" The tongue stud had vanished. She tinkled laughter.

Fighting an onset of light-headedness, George composed himself and took stock. However lovely, Polly was still a tease. To shatter any doubt, and with George halfway to crease, she produced a duck whistle from her absorbing cleavage. "Quack, quack." Sharing the blanket Ollie guffawed.

"Nice one, Pol", said Bridey cheerily and passed a packet of crisps for Henry and Lili to share.

"Come on, George," Henry shouted.

"Quack, quack."

There was a limit. From deep within himself boarding school resilience began coursing through George's veins. Instinctively he held himself a tad taller, put his shoulders back, and puffed out his chest. It was pure bravado.

Still in at the non-strikers end Jerzy rubbed a tender spot on his ribs and became inquisitive. "You know that bit of totty?"

George shrugged. "Middle," he called, taking his guard.

"Middle it is," said Herbert. "Five to come."

George excavated a trench, set his jaw in grim determination.

"Good luck, George," said Big Doug.

First up, Ken pitched the ball short, almost at the point of his follow through. It reared viciously at George's throat. He jerked out the way avoiding it, but was helpless as his falling cap nearly knocked a bail. Taking a deep breath he dusted down the Belters' badge and reset himself as Ken rolled in again.

"Footwork, footwork, soft hands, soft hands," George reminded himself. He stepped across to off stump and carved. Twack! A startled Wickham clattered wings in the copper beech as the ball disturbed adjacent leaves. Herbert scowled and raised both arms in the air. Six. Ken kicked the turf. George did a bit of gardening and retook his guard.

The next ball, after several gravestone ricochets, had Pitchforkers rabbiting around the churchyard. Six more.

"Posh boy, you hero!" Polly was clearly taking an interest in the battle. Ollie glared daggers.

Framed by the French windows Aunt Frances and Joy were agog. Rising out of his garden bench Sir Robert clapped his pleasure. "Well played, young man!" Mel whooped. In next and padding up, Delvin was in a state of prayer.

Fifth ball of the over Ken decided on a change of approach. He aimed fast and wide of off stump. Rocking back on his heels George flashed hard. Whack. The top edge flew over Radley in the slips like a tracer bullet into the stream.

"Fishing net!" Henry laughed.

"Wedgy, fetch." At Polly's command the lump of canine muscle bounded away and found itself pursued by a duet of yaps and barks.

"Porthos! Oohoo, oohoo!"

Crease bounds, George bellowed "Lobb!" which wasn't helpful in the least.

Having the head start Wedgy was first to dive, legs splayed, into the water. Re-emerging ball in mouth the dog had a good shake and gave its booty a triumphant chew. Then began a variation of the game of chase. It was too much for the Pitchforkers. They split their sides. "Only in the West Country," wheezed Radley, "can a pack of hounds stop play."

Order restored, and the dogs panting happily under guard, Ken returned to his business. He wiped the slobbery, pockmarked leather on his immaculate whites. Aware of a crumbling reputation he only had one delivery left of his allotted spell to make amends. He fluffed it. Maybe the ball's aerodynamics had gone awry or maybe it just slipped out of his fingers. Whichever it was, a rank full toss headed down leg.

In the zone, George aimed instinctively for cow-cum-pig corner. Fractionally late on the shot he held the pose and gulped. Arrowed towards the billiard room the ball had landed short with a noise that sounded like 'ponk'. He sank over his bat.

Mid pitch, Ken stood hands on hips and snorted with mirth. The reluctant Herbert signalled another six. Attracted by an onset of perspiration a fly buzzed passed George's nose. There followed several seconds of blissful skylark song and burbling water. Then Aunt Frances wailed. "You brute! You've murdered Hobbs!"

"Way to go, George," said Big Doug.

George gave a groan of despair. Whatever sustaining adrenalin rush he had dissipated.

On the grass in front of the French windows the tortoise hidden in its shell was inert as a half coconut. Finger prods from some helpful observers seemed to confirm Aunt Frances' original diagnosis.

Taking a deep breath George left his bat resting against his stumps and walked abjectly across the outfield, receiving a sympathetic pat on the back from Billy.

"Oops-a-daisy, posh boy!" said Polly, who with Ollie's help was holding on to Wedgy's straining collar.

"G-O T-O H-E-L-L," George mouthed silently to her as he stomped by preparing his apology to Aunt Frances. Sir Robert had already sacrificed his *Times*. Its quick crossword not in any way complete, the newspaper was respectfully laid over the casualty. Straightening upright he and George exchanged the briefest of pleasantries as Aunt Frances in high dudgeon and silently scooped up Hobbs. Meekly followed by Porthos she disappeared in Nettlegot's bowels. Lobb the Duckdog whined. Appearing calm, Hammond seemed to be coping very well – unlike George.

His stomach queasy, he helplessly watched Aunt Frances depart when a comforting hand squeezed his shoulder. "These things happen," said Delvin. "It beggars belief that the Lord moves in such mysterious ways. Do you happen to know who drained my hip flask? There's hardly the dregs left for a furtive swig. Go on, get back to the crease and put on a display for the maiden holding the Staffordshire. She fancies you rotten."

George had an onset of whooziness that stayed with him for the remainder of his innings, which was one ball. Billy fist-pumped a half-tracker that gated the Belter skipper. Called upon, Big Doug's finger straightened.

"Quack, quack."

The hosts were six wickets down. "Bloody great," mumbled Jerzy, at the non-strikers end. "No pressure on me, then." He patted the lucky rabbit's foot in the pocket of his whites. As he did so there was an almighty crash of breaking glass.

Taking umbrage Hairy Fred kicked out to clang a rail causing Billy to trot over on a mission to soothe bull, pig and Mel. "Somebody's thrown their toy's out of the pram," Radley smirked.

Skipping to the wicket Delvin ushered Jerzy for a quick word. "George has just bunged his bat through a billiard room window – smashed it to smithereens."

"What a numpty," Jerzy opined. "How ...?"

"Said he was aiming for a pile of blazers ... sweaty gloves. Hope it isn't because of something I said. Anyway, no real damage done to life and limb. I've asked Henry and Bridey to help pick a myriad of shards off the spare tortoise. I'll try hanging around for a bit and tough it out best I can."

It was wishful thinking on Delvin's part. Forthwith, the vicar chipped a charitable donation back to the bowler. Then Old Willy came and went without laying willow on leather. Fortuitously, Ollie survived the hat trick ball to pinch a single with an edge that nutmegged Radley. The Belters had reached a hundred. There was a real possibility of Jerzy carrying his bat.

"This pad's lost a strap," Keen Kev lamented, clucking like a hen over a broken egg and distracted from thinking up a window quote. Glass crackled under his feet, scratching the floor, and he was in the way of Joy's broom.

"There's binder twine in the scullery. Go and find it," said Joy, about to fly off the handle. "And I wouldn't be too long, if I were you."

A Belters' cheer greeted Jerzy's paddle sweep that brought up his fifty. The sound carried to reach Keen Kev who in that moment was in awe of a Lazarus. Held under a scullery tap of cold running water Hobbs winked. "My sweetheart," cooed Aunt Frances, Porthos neglected for once.

"Howzat!"

"Shit, shit, shit." Twineless Keen Kev hurried for bat and gloves, the loose pad flapping like a crippled wing. Excitement and nerves allied themselves. This was his hour. The one he had practised for with his India rubber ball. He scuffled passed Sir Robert kicking up a fuss, and passed a doleful George. News of the resurrection can wait, thought the number eleven. It was absolutely nothing to do with him.

Ollie broke off giving Polly reasons for his demise to wish Keen Kev good luck, then said something about being given a wide berth that made her laugh, but half-heartedly. Her sympathies lay with George.

"Cor, look what hobbit the cat's dragged in," said Radley when Keen Kev took middle guard.

"I reckon he's grave robbed W.G. Grace." The boundary holler from Ken was within Sir Robert's earshot.

He grabbed his binoculars. "Good God! George! What's the matter with you? First you commit tortoise genocide, then you become a bigger vandal than Birchtree and Furet put together, and if that not enough, you've let Furet endanger my grandfather's heirlooms. Explain how I had the misfortune to spawn you."

That was the last straw. Polly clenched her fists. She was back again on the estate she had left as a child. "Leave him alone, yer stupid old fart!"

Simultaneously, the ball leaving Billy's hand went wide of third slip for four byes. Big Doug hummed Faure's 'In Paradisum'. Radley commented on life in the doghouse. A pungent clamminess afflicted George's armpits and he went white as Griffin's sailcloth. Wellard snorted. And Sir Robert grasped his left arm in a manner worthy of the Snickworthy Players.

"Golly, have I missed something?" queried Aunt Frances, patting Hobbs dry with a tea towel.

Hers was not a singular surprise, however. Off a short run Billy bowled to Keen Kev. Willow flailed. Four. "Well done, Kev! Useful runs" Jerzy called down the wicket. A close blade inspection, however, marred Keen Kev's ecstasy. The splice had cracked ominously.

"Here's the one who put the snick in Snickworthy," Radley chirped. "Try again, Billy boy. Nasty, brutish and short, I think." Screwing up his eyes Ken Kev made another tentative back foot waft. Crump. The bat splintered asunder. "Howzat!" Radley pointed to a willow lump and a toppled bail. The match had reached the halfway stage. There was a hasty need to draw breath.

And, of course, scoff tea. It was the opportunity Barri had waited for. To his consternation, however, the Belters' 'secret weapon' was untouched.

"Think we were born yesterday?" said Radley, slapping the demijohn of Jerzy's 'apple juice'.

The necessity for a substitute had suddenly become paramount. Grabbing his skipper, Griffin sought permission to find someone fitting the bill. "Go, go," said George, flippantly. "I'm urgently wanted by Pater."

Things had become fractious.

The private lecture George endured accompanied by pieces of bat was about family loyalty and the importance of breeding. Letting standards slip was the easiest of things. Everybody else, Sir Robert said, could do what the hell they pleased. Being a Wimble-Clatt necessitated sacrifice, pig or no pig.

And there was one other thing – the distracting oik.

For their sins Polly and Wedgy were banished to the Church Lane stile – something that made Ollie want to get into the van and leave. "Lili will be disappointed," Polly persuaded, having already put her rolled up sheet of paper behind the van seats. No way did she want George to see her work now.

Henry, meanwhile, elevated Bridey and Lili onto Sir Robert's vacant bench, sparing them the glass fragments on the tartan blanket. Until she spotted bleeding Bridey thought Lili had been crunching on crisps. Guddling a bottle of claret Sir Robert slumped in his red leather armchair. There he would get regular updates from Joy confirming George was doing as he was told. And so far, it seemed, he was.

"No, Mel, absolutely not. And you can't persuade me otherwise." George was adamant. The new ball was Henry's to bowl with from the stream end, and no argument. And he himself would share it from the other. Ollie, he put to pasture at third man. Thumb on a pack of frozen peas and relegated to scoreboard gaffer loitered Barri. His sub patrolled long leg – a seismic fait accompli.

Sir Robert bellowed, negligent of his rising blood pressure. "I ban the bloody man myself along with that Furet cretin's father and my errant son does zero? Total insanity. All know Biggot's bent!"

"Not so much bent as Bobowskied, that's to say Mudworthed, really," Joy replied calmly, as if believing it explained everything. "Griffin had the brainwave and he did ask George ..."

"Our weeping carpenter?"

"Well yes, and he suggests Larry deserves another chance. We all want Mel to hang on to Wellard. And Larry loves cricket and he's only fielding, doing his bit."

"Oh, so it's 'Larry' now is it? You do know he's an adulterer."

Joy was unruffled. "And he so wants to talk to you alone after the match. Honestly he does. It's about Snickworthy Steep."

Sensing discord in the opposition ranks the Pitchforkers got run chase going with gusto. In doing so they chose a different target altogether. With a battle cry of "hit to the hobbit" Keen Kev was run ragged. The cause was obvious. Defensively, the Pitchforker openers had the measure of Henry. George, however, was biffed, nurdled and generally marmalised where they fancied.

Posted at long off Delvin chatted to Polly and they found themselves in total agreement – a rose garden would have enhanced Nettlegot nicely and George was being a stubborn "eejit".

The Belters captain remained resolute, however, in spite of Keen Kev again chasing leather in range of a Hairy Fred hoof. Surely luck would change. Maybe if he and Henry switched ends for an over? It was worth a try.

"Like scrumping apples from the tree," said Griffin, who in Big Doug's opinion had snaffled "a tickle". Henry had opened the door. For George, on the other hand, there was nothing but further sufferance, and he decided to revert to the stile end and be closer to Polly.

Mel pleaded in desperation. "Please, George, take a break. Let Ollie bowl. Please." She got a response.

"Delvin, turn your arm over from this end, will you," George ordered. "Perhaps, I could do with a rest."

Snickworthy's man of God shook his head in disbelief. "Me? You want me to bowl?"

"I do. And Jerzy will take over from Henry."

"You've told Jerzy this, of course?"

"Umm, not as yet," George confessed.

Delvin gave Polly a shrug and trotted away exercising his fingers.

Wonder of wonders, church practice proved fruitful and for Delvin things just clicked. Bamboozled by one turning sharply behind his legs to hit off peg Radley was fulsome with praise. "Garn, vicar that were a praper good 'un. Any time yer fancy a change of parish talk ter Ken."

"Providence," thought Delvin. By the end of his spell he was Mel's hero. Big Doug's finger ached from strenuous exercise and the game was prolonging beyond George's wildest imaginings.

Refreshing the scoreboard Barri clanged a metal-plated '7' on the nail below 'Wickets'. The Pitchforkers required nine runs to win and Ollie had yet to be interrupted from blowing Nettlegot Ned raspberries and making Lili daisy chains. Scenting the incredible, Belters had become mutinous, and not least Jerzy. When George took the ball, rubbed it on his whites and began marking his run up, Larry prowled muttering about the benefits of captains in chains and thrown away keys. Thankfully, Rupert's hand on Keen Kev's neck stopped the nervous giggling.

"For heaven's sake, George, don't be a complete ass," implored Delvin, pondering if his hip flask should have been left in the rectory. "Give the cherry to Ollie and quit showing-off, or you'll never hear the end of it."

Straddling the stile Polly also had something to say. "Bridey said you were a prat!" she heckled "I didn't believe her! Prove to me you ain't!" A bottom shuffled uneasily on Sir Robert's bench. And still George dithered.

"Who's he trying to impress?" said Henry, wanting answers. "And why pick Furet? Barmy if you ask me. Do you reckon it's blackmail?" He was not really being serious. At first and second slip he and Jerzy chewed their nails. They both agreed George had been acting strangely since the lunchtime of smoke rings mid week. Now he had become flaming irrational. Griffin clapped together his wicketkeeper's gloves. "George, hello!"

Waiting to face, his patience frayed, Billy became stroppy. "Them beasts can't be cooped up much longer. Are yer going to bowl at me or aren't yer, chapper? Make yer mind up. One way or another that pig's coming to Wiltshire."

Slowly Polly's voice penetrated and George came to his senses. Proverbially as lost as the Bumpkin he beckoned Ollie over. "I'm sorry. Here. Do your stuff." Humbly handing over the ball he threw Polly an uncertain smile that mixed apology with awkwardness.

In a mire of acute distress, the relief of seeing Ollie's fingers across the seam made Mel giddy.

A zephyr of wind ruffled the longer grass and flora at the boundary edge releasing a microscopic particle of pollen on a journey across the outfield. Eyes, though, were on Ollie bowling the game's penultimate over. Jerzy had kittens about having the last if push came to shove. Going for the yorker Ollie managed a full bunger. Billy slapped it. A single. Eight needed off a possible eleven balls. "Oh, god," said George. Ollie held up a hand in apology and reattempted the delivery. Leg stump cartwheeled.

Herbert stuck out an arm. "No ball."

"Bollocks it was, Herb," said Billy. "I was watching. I'm not having yer cheat no more. Behave." He called to his partner. "What d'yer want to do? Walk or stay put?" Ollie's emotions were put through the wringer.

The castled batter, with a show of dignity, stuck his willow under his arm and walked. Belters' jaws dropped. Scampering in from mid-wicket Mel gave Billy a hug before Ollie got a goluptious kiss on the cheek. "Oi, enough of that." Billy said. Eight down, and still eight runs required. It was even-stevens.

The new batsman was Ken. "Middle and leg," he said taking his guard before passing on a message to Billy. "Your dad says 'we're not here to mess about'."

"Is this a game of cricket or 'Happy Families'," quipped Griffin, clapping his gloves. "C'mon Ollie lad, another wicket if you will."

His first delivery Ken played defensively. The next Ollie slightly overpitched outside off stump allowing Ken to drive. But it was as if he had a butter pat for a bat and he clothed it. Yet, what should only have been a single became a fortuitous two. Keen Kev had got in a tangle.

Five to win, but a four would tie the match. And every Belter knew the rules. Ollie was the butt of advice. He looked to Polly. She gestured with a hand and finger to pitch it short. Ollie nodded his understanding and ran in. Deciding on 'see-ball-hit-ball' Ken heaved his bat.

"Yours Henry!" was the shout.

"Yep," said Ken setting off for a run before the ball sailed straight and true into a safe pair of hands. Nine down. The batsmen, though, had crossed to leave Billy on strike for the last ball of the over. Would he take a risk? Tenterhooks.

Ollie gave Mel a thumbs-up. "If we win I'm buying you all the colours of the rainbow for that hair of yours," said Mel, trying to put on a brave face.

"Cor, wouldn't that be a sight," said Ollie. Then looking towards Wellard he yawned with anxiety and opted to follow instinct. That included ignoring George's advice.

The ball Ollie delivered pitched on off stump and held its line. Perhaps, it bounced more than Billy expected. Whatever, it became a skier. "Catch!" screamed Mel. "Please." A spectator, Barri relived a nightmare.

"Two!' called Billy, starting to run.

"Mine!" shouted Griffin, back-peddling.

Larry, though, was already lumbering in from long leg. "I've got it."

There was a frantic yell from George. "Larry! Leave it!"

"Oh, bugger," said Old Willy.

Wellard oinked in possible agreement towards the inevitable.

Mel tripped over the verge of tears. "You wazzocks!" Griffin and Larry had collided and lay prostrate in the position colloquially known as 'sixty-nine'."Flipping fudge,' breathed Henry. "George, don't let either of them move."

Now seeing what Henry saw George squawked. "Griffin! The-ball's-in-the-small-of-your-back-stay-absolutely-still!"

"Strewth, two more," called Billy just as the tickly airborne speck was sniffed into Griffin's left nostril.

Mel, her eyes, like Griffin's, wells of water, was galloping unfocused as the Belters stand-in keeper convulsed. The sneeze was irreversible. "Argh-arghhh-choooo." The weight of the ball disappeared and Griffin gave a hapless groan.

Having scampered one, Billy turned for the second that would tie the game.

"No!" wailed Mel, falling to her knees, head buried. "Wellard!" she sobbed.

Click. "'Owzat, umpire?" Old Willy asked the question of Herbert.

Billy picked himself up, dusted his shirt and pads with a batting glove and thumped the pitch with willow.

The lightest of touches fell upon Mel's heaving shoulder. She looked up blurrily. "'Tis alright, my dove," said Old Willy undoing the knotted, wyvern embroidered tie from about his waist. "I reckon you can put this around the neck of that pig. 'Cos he's staying in Somerset."

"Bravo!" shouted Aunt Frances.

"Wahay!" Joy cheered.

"Well," said Old Willy looking around at his teammates, "there was no point me just standing and gawking like you lot. Seems like I'm the only Belter true to the name." Then he beamed.

George kissed the cannonball and crossed bats on his cap and was almost lost for words. "Willy, wow, that throw was amazing!" He was less generous to Ollie who rolled on the pitch laughing "gerroff, gerroff" as Wedgy tried to lick his face and Lili scragged his tummy. Both Bridey and Polly, George noticed, were absorbed in Henry. Shortly, Mel had joined them. "Sminky, I'll always be Sminky," George lamented self-pityingly.

Oblivious to George's demons, Jerzy was effusive. "Told you my rabbit's foot was lucky!"

"It wasn't your throw that hit the stumps," said Rupert putting an arm around Jerzy's shoulder.

"No, but I willed it to."

Ambling over Billy outstretched a hand. "Fair play. If memory serves me right Mel's won herself a shaggy old bull." On this occasion the blacksmith's was the only mouth falling open.

Where the Pitchforkers clustered there was a smaller exchange. "Ta, Herb," said Radley, lighting a presented cigar before having a chat to Rupert.

Meanwhile, Sir Robert opened another bottle of claret and prepared to hold court.

TWENTY-EIGHT

Bat Room

There were high spirits under the broken-antlered stag. "Don't be a plonker," laughed Ollie, rebuffing Barri's notion of him using sheep shears instead of hair clippers. "Here you go," said Polly arriving. "Three pints of I don't quite know what."

A smoke ring dispersed, and Jerzy nearly toppled off his bar stool – the bop on the arm earned for spitting into Old Willy's scrumpy pint, ironically of Jerzy's own making. Beside them, loud and legless, Keen Kev slurred his finest moments to Delvin and Joy.

"Reckon Little Kev would have done better today than Keen Kev," chuckled Rupert admiring his stuffed badger. "I'm glad Ollie proved himself a good egg. But bloody hell, George, you were out of control. What got into you? Delvin thinks it was his apple brandy."

George gave a sheepish shrug and bibbled his ale. "Don't be too harsh on Kev. His runs were vital." Managing a chuckle he nodding a greeting at Larry and Daphne who guddled merrily with Griffin. Then his eyes lingered again on Polly.

The Burning Stump heaved in celebration. Behind the bar Bridey smiled and smiled. Having selected a suitable plectrum from his wallet and loosened his favoured maroon cravat, dark horse Henry strummed his guitar and sung to the tune of 'We Are The Champions', making the words up as he went along.

"I've swung my bat
And … bowled cricket balls
I've borne pheasants and … scrumpy and the 'Folly' that flows from it
My thanks to Zum …
We are the Belters,
We are the Belters,
And we'll be keeping Wellard to the end…
Everybody!"

And, apart from a couple of 'furriners' that 'passed' on it, the catchy chorus was roared emotionally by one and all. They were the Belters and *their* pig was staying put.

"Speech!" bellowed Big Doug. "Come on, Mel, a few words are in order!"

"Mel! Mel! Mel! Mel!" arose the chant.

Crimson and standing to a huge cheer Mel stammered an incoherent bounty of thanks that concluded with Hairy Fred's gratitude to Henry. With relief she plonked herself back down next to Billy. "Well, 'tis been a long day," said Radley across the corner table. "I think I'll go up and leave yer lovebirds to it. I'll see yer bright and early, Billy boy."

"Right yer are, Dad. Night night."

They watched him leave. His and Billy's rooms were 'on the house'. Billy gave a heavy sigh. "He's praper knackered. The cancer's eaten the life outta him. And the farm's too much fer just me. We have to sell up. Soft bugger's kept Hairy Fred since a calf. Promised Mum he would. Last thing she asked, it was. Never thought to sell him. Just wanted him to have a good home. Neither of us could think how to give him that when ... well, then that daft car of yours popped a tyre. Sized you up as a praper caring sort, he did. Not that I didn't give him few hints."

"Pull the other one, its got bells," she mocked. Then toying with a beer mat she became earnest. "Billy, can I you ask you summat?"

"Fire away."

"Rupert said..." Her chin quivered. "He said he thought you were in, that you beat Old Willy's throw. Where you in? Tell me the truth."

There was a moment's hesitation. "Our Herbert's been known to make mistakes."

Mel stared deeply into Billy's eyes and he was unsuccessful in avoiding her gaze. "Like I said," he eventually murmured, "you're the caring sort." Impulsively, she snogged him.

Another was also enjoying physical contact. In the dark of the Wellcombe Cottage log shed Flirty Bertie, home alone, was leaping, growling, mooing and claw-swiping. Carrying a scratch, a leader amongst the harassed colony of pipistrelles took to leathern wings and chonked its fellows to follow. It was best to seek alternative accommodation – somewhere more appropriate for a mating roost.

Sunshine streamed through a gap in the thin curtains and shone on the oar's golden lettering and the blackcurrant berries decorating the wall. The intimacy that was Angela beguiled Henry. His travel alarm clock said six-thirty. He stretched, yawned, and opened a leaded light to intensify the birdsong. Swinging a leg out of the bed he accidentally knocked his guitar. It had been some night. Later, he would have plenty to put in his Moleskine. Tomorrow, George was going to organise four ewes for him. He would name them Miss Alley, Miss McColl, Miss Gimblett, and Miss Kitchen. Now, though, he debated – reread a few pages of his self-sufficiency bible, make a cup of instant coffee or admire Folly Farmyard's first resident animal? It was a no-brainer.

Throwing open Angel's door he bade good morning to Hairy Fred. "Can I offer you breakfast, sir? There's grass or whatever Auntie Mel's prepared. Ah, as I thought, you would like to try Auntie Mel's. A sound choice, sir. If you'll excuse me a tick, I believe she's left it in the barn."

Henry strolled to get the tub of grain and discovered other arrivals.

"Fantastic. Bats!" Wanting a closer look he quietly climbed a wooden ladder found lying amongst old straw and made a discovery. The corner of a polythene bag poked just visible from a deep wall niche that once upon a time would have supported a thick beam. Giving the bag a tug Henry got a surprise. "Blimey, this really will make you lot go blind." he exclaimed to his new visitors. The bag contained lurid girlie magazines. "Bet George would like to see these."

Then he gave the pipistrelles a forewarning. "Don't start thinking you're staying. I'll be out this evening with a broom."

Nettlegot was having a fraught start to the week.

"Remarkable," said Aunt Frances staring up at the hole in the billiard room ceiling. "Rare and remarkable. I've just sent your ghastly Furet man away. We can't have him fix the glass. Not yet."

Sir Robert was profoundly irritated. "What can we do? I should have asked George to put cling film or cardboard over the window on Saturday evening."

"Well, Robert, you didn't. You tied yourself up with Biggot. Poor old you, I can't believe what he said happened to Rosemary." She crumbled a sparkle of reds, blues and blacks between her thumb and middle finger. "Pipistrelle poo, I'd say. Saw similar once at a friend's in Kew. They will move of their own accord. Eventually. But I suggest your cricket teas are al fresco for the time being. Some sort of gazebo will do for changing purposes."

"I'll be damned if ..."

"Robert, Robert, Robert, listen to me. Bats of the wild variety aren't allowed to be disturbed. That's the law."

"Humph! So how long do I have to suffer this confounded safari park?"

"September ... probably. So, meantime, I might as well help the vicar organise the white elephant."

TWENTY-NINE

Fête Full Day

Wickham socialised with the India runner ducks that quacked in a fold of wicker hurdles under the copper beech. Strategic straw bales arranged, George stuck assorted stumps into the ground to form a rough circle. Already, Ollie, Polly, Bridey and Lili had soaked themselves apple bobbing.

Well into the merry month of May and the cricket field was given over to church fund raising. Delvin had finally got around to doing his part in appeasing the bishop who, in turn, had torn up accusatory missives. A generous donation from Aunt Frances had covered the restoration of the hunky punk and she was now on the warpath providing Vera Scragg with a tough interview. There was to be no question of boundary nets.

Having spotted a handsome delight park a red sports car Margie played with her gold bangle and burned with curiosity. "Mrs Dapling? Who's that over by the tombola talking to Doug Birchtree?"

On the drinks stall Mrs Dapling carried on pouring blackcurrant squash into plastic cups with one hand and rocking a pram with her other. "The new doctor. I think his name's David Fester. Gilly Criddle says he's bought the Olde Bakery."

"Single?"

"Can't see a ring, dear. Can you? Though, these days that doesn't count for much."

"Joy Budd's showing."

Margie tittered. "Delphiniums in the flower show?"

"Preggers, dear." Mrs Dapling wiped up an inadvertent slosh with a tissue. "Are you still locking Mr Furet out of his cottage?"

"I'd never do that!" snorted Margie, sounding self-righteously indignant. "I just don't leave it open when I'm out. I'd always let him in if I'm there."

"I think you ought to speak to him, dear. You can see he's over by the stream trying to organise the duck race. Those dogs love his squirrel tail. Your mother's told me, not that I'd speak to her of course, that Mr Furet's been to see Larry Biggot. We don't want any more unpleasantness, do we? But well done on your planning permission, that was a surprise to everybody."

"The planning officer and a couple of councillors – friends of Daddy – worked so hard for me. I was very grateful."

"That explains it – the cars outside Mr Furet's cottage. Oh. I almost forgot to pass the message. My hubby's happy to sell you a bit land for your horse. He says you only have to ask. Quite honestly I don't know what's got into him."

"Thank you, Mrs Dapling. That's wonderful. Really, really kind. Er, how much is your squash?"

It was action stations.

Hassling a blackbird Margie hopped over the stile to go and change her blouse, dispose of her bra, and grab an ice cube from the fridge. What she planned was unsubtle, but she believed it enough to get results from most men. The ruse had worked amazingly on Jerzy using a half pint of bitter shandy. Now a mere 5p invested in a cup of blackcurrant squash would add extra colour to the sacrifice of a slightly threadbare white blouse. Practice cut the overheads.

Her target loomed at the coconut shy where Barri browsed his 'Wisden'. Quickly before it melted she applied the ice. Then she gave a purposeful barge. Purple wetness sloshed across her bosom to reveal stimulating pertness. "Oooo, silly me." Margie looked coquettishly upwards. "It's David isn't it?"

"Daffyd. Daffyd Mester. I'm sorry, I don't think we've…"

"I'm Margie B… Margie Mudworth. "It's like an invasion." She giggled. "I'm guessing you're from Wales."

"Patagonia, actually. It's a long story. You'll have to put that top in the washing machine pretty smartish."

"Can I use yours?" She jiggled wantonly.

"Absolutely. Best sooner rather than later."

Her prey snared, Margie dropped a key into Barri's lap. "Barri sweetie, give this to Kevin, will you? It's for his back door," she simpered. "And get your act together with Joy."

"Yeah, Margie. Whatever. I promise to be good." He looked up, and gasped. "Flaming heck!"

The good doctor administered modesty with the gallant sacrifice of his linen jacket.

Happily, on the cricket front there was also news of an opener brought to Mel and Griffin manning the white elephant stall. "Old Willy's just rung with a Zum update," reported George, "Sunny Gavaskar is making his Championship debut against 'Glawster' today. Bet you didn't know this – Sunny reckons there's stark resemblance between the Taunton dressing room and the Black Hole of Calcutta. Also, apparently, dogs shatter his composure. The ones here shatter mine. Anyway, Beefy's been making hidden woofs. Oh, and Henry's offered us the old hen house as the Belters temporary changing room."

"You are joking?" choked Griffin.

"Not a bit. It's really funny. His Cuckoo Marans prefer the camper van. So he says he can tidy the house up. With some hardboard over the chook hatches and a lick of paint it'll be hunky-dory. The old Fordson can lug it over. Must dash and put a 'No Entry' sign on the French windows. Pater doesn't want anybody trying to get in to frighten the bat babies whilst he does the duck herding."

"The pleasures of Zum bats and Belters, eh, George," quipped Griffin, deadpan.

"What?"

"Never mind."

Mel poked Griffin with her elbow once George was out of range. "Do you think he knows we know about the mags?"

"Nah. But I'm sure he's going to be eager to please for a while. And at least Keen Kev's lost clout." Griffin wrinkled his nose. "Seen this tea cosy he's donated? It's absolutely disgusting. I say we abandon ship and go and watch Sir Robert and Lobb."

Mel needed no second invitation.

"Pity Billy can't be here because of the auction," she said as she strolled. It seemed, though, everyone else was. "Hey, have a gander at Henry. He's covered in muck and he's still got his cravat. Yay, George is on his way." She beamed at almost every familiar face. The Belters were like an onion, she thought, bonded and made out of layers. The Bumpkin Crew were the core. The successive layers were old and growing friends. The new blood of Timmy Dapling was there as well. And the outer layer Keen Kev could keep for himself. Now the nonsense had gone away she at least allowed him a sympathetic smirk.

Wearing his traditional smock and straw hat Sir Robert hollered, his voice carrying like a town crier. "Duck herding! Duck herding! Roll up! Roll up and witness the feats of Lobb the Duckdog! This amazing dog will herd the ducks here in these hurdles, around those straw bales and into that pen of cricket stumps in under three minutes!"

"What rubbish, innit, Griff?" said Mel. "Lobb won't do it under five. Betcha me pig."

Epilogue

Sharing an unsteady table outside the Mitre Tavern, the oldest pub in Melbourne, three aging people had a reunion. Brushed-up well Bindy divvied out fags to Ted and Edna. "Goes without saying, none of us would be sat here if Tadeus Bobowski hadn't shot that scabby stag for his stew. I've said it over and over. We couldn't have let it rot, could we? Yer were right, Ted, to have had a go. Wasn't yer fault it was Lady Doo-dah in that car. But she recognised both of yer. I had to bump her off." She cackled. "The sloe gin was a lovely touch, Edna, yer naughty cockroach. But gawd, Ted, yer bucket of sheep's blood was monstrous."

They crowed with mirth until Bindy collapsed in a fit of coughing.

"Look on the bright side," she said, once recovered, "the girl Margie's up and coming. And I'll keep tabs on her. She could yet put us right. It's not too late to get back what's ours. So stop blaming yerself about Kevin, Edna. It was just the phase of the moon."

The Belters would have to battle, again, while the scruffbags of Zum marched on to further glory.